THE LAN
STAMP C

About

David Rennie first star... at the age of about nine, he was given a collection by an older cousin. That was over thirty years ago, and he has never lost his interest. After spending most of his National Serice at the NATO HQ in Oslo, he embarked on a career in management and administration which finally led to a directorship with a publishing company. However times were tough and in 1979 after twelve years with the company he was made redundant.

It was then that his lifelong interest in stamps proved its worth. Using the redundancy money and a large part of his own collection, plus experience from many years dealing with Philatelic auctioneers, he set up his own business – BLACK SWAN POSTAL SALES – running monthly postal sales with lots made up to suit collectors and small dealers. Although he now sees more stamps than ever, they continue to hold their fascination for him.

Also in this series

THE LANGUAGE OF STAMP COLLECTING

David Rennie

Star

A STAR BOOK
published by
the Paperback Division of
W. H. ALLEN & Co. Ltd

A Star Book
Published in 1982
by the Paperback Division of
W.H. ALLEN & Co. Ltd
A Howard and Wyndham Company
44 Hill Street, London W1X 8LB

Printed and bound in Great Britain by
Mackays of Chatham Ltd

Typeset in Great Britain by
Sunrise Setting, Torquay, Devon

ISBN 0 352 31088 X

Note to readers: Cross-references are given in italics.

Introduction

One of the reasons why stamp collecting is such a fascinating pastime is that there is so much to learn and discover that one can never hope to know it all. Just keeping up with modern technical developments and the myriad of new issues is an immense task in itself, let alone finding out all that has gone before. Despite the vast store of information already published in catalogues, magazines and books, there is still a need for collectors, and particularly new collectors, to be able to find out quickly the meaning or explanation of all the terms and expressions which are in general use and which may puzzle them.

There is nothing more disheartening than to read an article in a magazine, or to talk to a dealer or another collector and to find words are used which are a mystery. My aim in writing this book, therefore, was to provide as comprehensive a listing as possible, not only of the technical words, but also of many of the colloquial expressions, nicknames, etc. which a collector may see or hear, and to provide a concise explanation of them. Since postal history and picture postcard collecting are also growing in popularity and are more and more overlapping stamp collecting, I have included many expressions which are used in these areas also.

The book is not intended to be a technical manual of printing processes, perforation techniques, specialist philately or post office procedures and machinery. Rather it is the stepping stone by which the collector can pass from ignorance to awareness with the minimum of difficulty. All words printed in *italics* have individual entries of their own, and in addition many cross references are provided which by reading will provide a greater understanding. With knowledge comes enjoyment and appreciation. I therefore hope that as a result of referring to this book you will be able to more fully enjoy stamp collecting in general and your own collection in particular.

— David Rennie
London
December 1981

BIBLIOGRAPHY

The ABCs of Stamp Collecting, Booklet, Scott Publishing, NY, USA (1973).

Collect British Stamps, Colin Narbeth, Lutterworth Press, London, UK (1969).

Collecting Stamps, Paul Villiard, Doubleday and Co., NY, USA (1974).

The Philatelist's Companion, Bill Gunston, David and Charles, Newton Abbot, UK (1975).

Philatelic Terms Illustrated, Russell Bennett and James Watson, Stanley Gibbons, London, UK (1978).

Picton Postcard Catalogue, Ron Mead, Joan Venman, Dr. J.T. Whitney, BPH Publications, Chippenham, UK (1981).

The Postal History of Great Britain and Northern Ireland, R.M. Willcocks, London, UK (1972).

Stamp Collecting, Stanley Philips, Stanley Gibbons, London, UK (1965).

A Start to Stamp Collecting, Kenneth Chapman, W. Foulsham & Co. Ltd, Slough, UK (1969).

The International Encyclopedia of Stamps, IPC Magazines, London, UK (1971).

Picture Postcards and Their Publishers, Anthony Byatt, Golden Age Postcard Books, Malvern, UK (1978).

All recognised catalogues.

Abnormal. Certain surface printed stamps of Great Britain of the period 1862–80. They come from plates, or in colours, not normally issued for postal use, but which were prepared for registration at Somerset House and have subsequently found their way into collectors' hands.

Accumulation. A term used by auctioneers and dealers to describe a lot which may contain loose stamps; stamps in packets, envelopes, tins or boxes; stamps in albums, on loose album leaves or stock cards; covers, postcards and ephemera, etc. They are usually assembled together in an untidy fashion in a box or container, sometimes of one country but more usually of many.

Acknowledgement of Receipt. A stamp issued against payment of a special fee so that acknowledgement of receipt of the postal item will be obtained. Mostly countries collect such fees using normal postage stamps and attach a suitable *etiquette* to the envelope (see *recorded delivery*).

Adhesive. 1) The gum by which means a stamp may be affixed to the envelope. 2) The name given to a stamp having adhesive (gum) on the back thus distinguishing it from a stamp embossed on postal stationery or a meter frank.

Advertisement. Some stamps have been issued having an advertisement printed on the back. The most well known are certain Queen Victoria issues of New Zealand, but some British stamps were also printed experimentally. Modern self-adhesives from Sierra Leone have advertisements printed on the backing paper. Sometimes known as "Adson".

Advertisement Pane. More common than advertisements on stamps these are booklet *panes* which contain advertisements on labels *se-tenant* with the postage stamps. Collectors try to assemble complete collections of panes which have different advertisements although the stamps may be the same.

Aerogramme. A special lightweight single sheet of paper printed and gummed and designed when sealed to form an air letter. The official ones carry a printed stamp and they sometimes attract a special lower airmail rate.

Airmail. A general term to denote letters and postal items carried by air. The cost is usually more than for surface mail particularly on the longer distances, and of course the time taken is much less than by surface mail. Many countries produce special "airmail" stamps for use on such items.

Airgraph. Used by British Forces in the Middle East during World War II. A special printed form was used for the message and the recipient's address. This when completed was photographed and the negative flown to the appropriate post office. Here a print was made which was then delivered to the addressee in the normal way. A similar service known as "V" Mail was in use for United States' Forces.

Albino. A stamp or overprint which due to lack of ink shows as a colourless impression only.

Album. A book, in which collectors arrange and mount their stamp collections for order and protection. There are many different types, some with plain leaves, others part printed by country or fully printed with spaces for each stamp issued. Albums may be fully bound or loose leaf: Spring back, peg-fitting or spring-clip, etc.

Alphabet. Great Britain's first issues had coloured letters printed in the bottom corners. These, over a period of time, came from four sets of hand punches having distinctive type-faces, commonly known as Alphabets I, II, III, IV and which enable collectors to more closely identify individual stamps.

Aniline. Stamps printed with ink containing aniline are generally brighter than would otherwise be the case, and have the ink suffused on the surface and showing through to the back. The term aniline is sometimes used to describe stamps having aniline characteristics in their finished appearance although the true aniline substance may not have been present in the ink.

Appliqué. A category of picture postcard on which additional material has been added to the basic printing, such as glitter, hair, cloth, etc.

Approval Dealers Protection Society (ADPS). These initials in an advertisement or on a letter heading signify membership of the Society which provides various services for approval dealers.

Approvals. Stamps or covers sent to a collector for his consideration prior to purchase and which in the event of non-purchase must be returned to the dealer within a specified time. Approvals may be supplied by country, theme or other collecting area and can be graded in price or according to the collector's requirements i.e., suitable for beginner, for a specialist etc. They are usually contained in special small-sized booklets suitable for transmission through the post.

Army Post Office (APO). The organisation responsible for handling soldiers' mail. Generally such mail can be recognised by the distinctive postmarks which usually have the letters "APO", "FPO" or some other inscription.

ASDA. Indicates membership of either the American or the Australian Stamp Dealers Association.

Arrow Block. An arrow-shaped mark appears in the margin of many modern stamps as an aid for postal clerks when dividing sheets into halves or quarters. An arrow block is a marginal block of four stamps with the full arrow in the margin.

ASCAT. International Association of Publishers of Stamp Catalogues.

As Is. An expression used by auctioneers and dealers to indicate that the lot or stamp is sold without their usual guarantee and therefore is not returnable. The expression does not necessarily mean that the item is not genuine, merely that the dealer, perhaps because of lack of knowledge, is unable to express a definite opinion and the buyer must make his own decision and act accordingly.

Auction. A method of sale whereby stamps are made up into lots which are then offered for sale to the highest bidder on a particular day. A detailed catalogue is produced and viewing arrangements are provided. Strictly speaking, an auction should be held in public, but there are many philatelic auctions which are run through the post, following the basic principles of a public auction. These are that the highest bidder shall be the purchaser, but at a price of one bidding step above the second highest bidder. The bidding steps and other terms and conditions should be printed in the catalogue. The auctioneer works through taking each lot in turn and calling for bids at a level which is determined by the present selling price "on the book", i.e. the price which has been bid prior to the sale by either the viewers or postal bidders. It is important to realise that this figure may not be the limit placed by the prior bidder and than any bids received "in the room" then compete with the book up to the limit set by the prior bidder. If the room bidders drop out, the book bidder will then buy at the next step above.

Back of the Book (BOB). A term used by some dealers and auctioneers to refer to postage dues, official stamps, fiscal and revenue stamps etc. which appear in the catalogue after the main listing of general postage stamps, i.e. at the back of the book.

Backstamp. A handstamp (usually *circular date stamp*) applied to the back of a postal item to indicate the date it was received either at a transit office or at the office of final destination. On a much travelled cover the various transit marks, etc., will enable the collector to chart the route and timetable of the letter to its destination.

Balloon Post. Usually refers to letters carried by balloon out of Paris, which was besieged, during the Franco-Prussia War 1870–2. Also to letters from Przmysl which was besieged by the Russians during World War I. Ballon monté indicates that the balloon was manned. Ballon non monté that it was unmanned. There are many philatelic balloon posts, i.e. special balloon flights which carried covers for publicity or profit.

Bank Lot. A dealer's description for a mixed selection of stamps on paper as received from bank mail. They are better quality than *kiloware* since they contain stamps from all over the world usually with higher values from registered and airmail correspondence.

Bantam. A popular name given to reduced size stamps, especially those of South Africa, issued during World War II to conserve paper stocks, also the British halfpenny stamps of 1870 and to certain halfpenny stamps of the Australian states etc. Usually two bantam-sized stamps are equal to one normal sized stamp.

Bâtonné. A special paper, either woven or laid, having a watermark of straight lines spaced so as to form a guide for handwriting.

Bilingual. A stamp having two languages printed on it to meet the needs of mixed populations speaking different languages within one country, common examples being the stamps of Belgium and South Africa.

Bilingual Pair. A *se-tenant* pair of stamps each printed in a different language. For example English and Afrikaans on the stamps of South and South-West Africa.

Binder. The outer part of a loose leaf album.

Bisect. A stamp cut in half and postally used, with the authority of the Post Office, usually because stamps of a particular denomination were unavailable. For example half of a twopenny was used as a penny in Guernsey. Bisects are best collected on cover (or at least a large piece). Make sure that the postmark ties the bisect across its cut edge to the cover or piece.

Bishop Mark. A circular mark struck on pre-stamp entires showing in abbreviated form the month and date on which they were posted or received in London. They were named after Henry Bishop who as first Postmaster General after the Restoration initiated their use in 1661.

Black Plate. A reference to a Great Britain Penny Red issued in 1841 and which was printed from one of the plates originally used to print the Penny Black.

Black Postcard. A propaganda postcard produced by the British government and generally attacking the German government, which were infiltrated into Germany during World War II.

Bleuté. See *Blued paper*.

Blind Cancellation. A postmark which either does not show any place name of origin (see *Dumb Cancellation*) or sometimes one which has a name but no date. This is due to the date slug being missing.

Blind perforation. Due to a defective perforating pin the hole in the paper has sometimes not been cut through, although it may show an impression of the pin.

Blind Stamp. An extra unprinted area of paper of stamp size left between two other stamps or between a stamp and the sheet margin. This was necessary in certain combinations of printing format and paper/perforation layouts. A somewhat risky practice, since it normally left watermarked paper available for the forger. Also known as *Interspace*.

Block. A group of four or more stamps still joined together from at least two vertical and two horizontal rows. If they form a perfect rectangle the block is said to be "regular", if not it is "irregular".

Block CA. Name for the watermark which has a redesigned crown and lettering, and was used by the Crown Agents from 1957. It superceded the Multiple Script CA watermark.

Blued, Bleuté. Many early stamps appear to be printed on blue or bluish paper. This blueing, which may vary considerably in shade and density, was caused by a chemical reaction between the damp paper and the ink during printing, possibly due to the presence of prussiate of potash. Do not confuse this with paper which was blue before the printing began.

Blue Safety Paper. 'Safety', here, is meant in the sense of security. This paper specifically had prussiate of potash added to it during the manufacture. The effect was to prevent the ink from penetrating very deeply, so that any attempt to remove the postmark removed the printed design as well.

Bogus. A fictitious stamp; sometimes a genuine stamp with a fictitious overprint or a stamp from a non-existent country (see *Forgery*).

Booklet. 1) A small booklet having stamps (and maybe advertising matter) bound in it. It is sold by the Post Office for the price of the stamps, sometimes from special vending machines. Swedish style booklets have the stamps stuck into the booklet by the *selvedge*, or the panes may be either sewn or stapled into position. When booklets were first introduced there was a nominal charge and usually one stamp was cancelled or replaced by a label (see *St Andrews Cross*) to represent the charge. 2) A book of assorted stamps made up by an approval dealer, or club member, for circulation, with a view to selling individual stamps or sets. Also known as approval books or club books.

Bourse. That part of a stamp exhibition or stamp fair where dealers set up their stands to sell to collecters. Also the period of time at the end of a club meeting when members sell stamps to each other.

Boxed. Description of a postmark, handstamp or *cachet* to indicate that it has an outer line around it, usually in the shape of a rectangle.

BPA Certificate. A certificate issued by an expert committee of the *British Philatelic Association* which indicates the genuineness or otherwise of a stamp or cover.

Bradbury Wilkinson and Co. (BW). One of the major stamp printers in Great Britain.

Bridger and Kaye Ltd (B&K). London stamp dealers who publish the Commonwealth Catalogue, normally referred to simply as the "Commonwealth" or "B&K".

Britannias. Popular name for the early issues of Barbados, Mauritius and Trinidad which show a seated figure of Britannia holding a spear.

British European Airways (BEA). After 1951 it issued its own airmail stamps to cover fees on letters carried. The letters had to be handed in and collected at airports and town terminals and were not carried by the Post Office.

British Forces Post Office (BFPO). Post Offices for members of the British Army and Royal Air Force. The Royal Navy uses the longer title of BFPO SHIPS.

British North America (BNA). A popular collecting area which includes Canada and its constituent states such as Newfoundland, British Columbia, New Brunswick, Nova Scotia, Prince Edward Island and Vancouver Island, and which also sometimes includes Bermuda although this is also included in British West Indies by many collectors.

British Philatelic Association (BPA). The use of the initials signifies membership of this association which is the ruling body for philatelic matters in Great Britain.

British West Indies (BWI). Popular collecting area which includes the Bahamas, Barbados, Bermuda (sometimes included in British North America), Jamaica, Belize, Guyana as well as the Leeward and Windward Islands' States, Trinidad etc.

Broken Frame. Description which indicates that part of the design forming the frame or outer edge of the stamp or the *vignette* has been damaged on the printing plate. This is visible on the printed stamp as a white break in the coloured line.

Broken Letter. Description of an overprint or surcharge which indicates that some damage to the printing plate has occurred causing malformed or broken letters. The presence of broken letters can very often enable a collector to identify the specific position on the sheet of the stamp.

Bullseyes. A popular name for the first stamps issued by Brazil which had large white numerals printed on a circular black background.

Burélage. A pattern of fine wavy lines or dots usually forming a network which was intended to make forgery of the stamp more difficult. The stamps were printed on burélage as a background.

Burrélé. Having *Burélage* incorporated into the design of a stamp or, in the case of Queensland, for example a band across the back of the stamp.

Cachet. Usually a handstamp (but sometimes printed) on a piece of mail providing further information concerning the circumstances in which it was posted, the route followed or the means of transport. This would include first flight, polar or other expeditions, zeppelin, Condor or balloon flights, etc. It can be applied privately or by the Post Office. It is not a postmark.

Calender. A machine fitted with rollers used for finishing the surface of paper using a combination of moisture, heat and pressure.

Cancel or Cancellation. Any mark stamped, written, printed or perforated across a stamp or printed postal stationery to prevent its re-use. It includes *postmarks* or *pen cancels* ; The words *cancelled* or *specimen* or other similar words; punched or torn holes and corners etc. A cancellation need not say anything or give any information, hence the considerable use in earlier times of *dumb cancellors* and *obliterators*.

Cancelled. When printed on a stamp it indicates that the stamp has either been issued as a *specimen* for official purposes, or more usually that the balance of stocks of that issue have been *remaindered* to the philatelic trade.

Cancelled To Order (CTO). Mint stamps printed with postmarks and sold to the philatelic trade at below face value. They may be either new issues or withdrawn stocks. Usually with modern CTOs only a quarter segment of the CDS appears in the corner, usually clearly printed but with little information since the object is to provide what purports to be a very *fine used* copy. Earlier issues may be found cancelled with black bars or other similar marks.

Cantonal Issues. The stamps issued prior to 1850 by some of the Cantons in Switzerland.

Cape Triangles. A popular name for the first stamps issued by the Cape of Good Hope which were triangular in shape.

Capped Numeral. Refers specifically to a deformed number "2" at the left on the 1890–93 2-cent Washington stamp issued by the United States of American. The effect when printed resembles a cap.

Cardboard. A printing medium heavier than paper used mainly for postcards. Sometimes used for taking proof impressions of printing plates, dies etc. It has also been used for postage stamps and, in the case of Russian issues in 1915, as currency in lieu of coinage. In this latter case, although the stamps were not authorized for postal use, some were, in fact, posted.

Caricature. Generally refers to the many parodies of the *Mulready Envelope* issued in 1840 to deride the Post Office and other establishment institutions. They were so effective that the

Mulready Envelopes were withdrawn after only a very short time in use.

Carlist Issues. Stamps issued in the Basque region of Spain during the second Carlist War, 1872–6, by supporters of Don Carlos, pretenders to the Spanish throne.

Cartologist. A picture postcard collector (also deltiologist).

Cartridge. A type of paper mainly used for drawing but also used extensively for album leaves. Very rarely used for stamps.

Castles. A popular name for the first series of high-value stamps issued in Great Britain in the reign of Queen Elizabeth II. Each value showed a castle, there being one each from England, Scotland, Wales and Northern Ireland together with the Wilding portrait of Her Majesty.

Catalogue. 1) A philatelic dealer's price list which gives additional information (in many cases extremely comprehensive information) about the stamps which it lists. Some catalogues deal in great detail with one country or even particular issues of one country. Others are more simplified and cover particular areas of the world. It follows that the more specialized a collector's interests the more specialized and comprehensive his catalogue should be.

2) An auctioneer's listing and description of the lots which comprise a particular auction. As in (1) above, some catalogues are sumptuously produced with much information and detail, photographs etc. and remain as works of reference long after the auction has taken place. Others are simpler and serve only to provide information to prospective buyers for a particular auction or sale after which they are usually discarded.

Catalogue Value (CAT or C). This is the price shown in a catalogue (which should always be specific as to publisher and date) for a particular stamp either in mint or used condition. Do not confuse this with the market value which will vary considerably depending upon factors such as condition, rarity, popularity of the country or issues concerned, current demand, method of purchase etc.

Catapult Mail. A ship-to-shore airmail service used by the French and Germans on transatlantic mail, the aeroplane being catapulted into the air when the ship was about 5–600 miles from land. A special fee was paid and the letters suitably endorsed.

Censor. In time of war, letters, especially forces' mail, may be opened and censored before transmission overseas. Such letters are postmarked (the censor mark) to show that this has taken place, or may be resealed using a special censor label. Censors were issued with specific numbers, with handstamps and labels to match, and thus collectors are able to identify where and when the censor acted.

Centred, Centring. The position of the stamp design in relation to the perforations of the stamp. Ideally there will be the same size margin left and right, and similarly top and bottom. If not then the stamp is not correctly centred. The words left, right, top and bottom or the compass points are used to indicate in a description where the design is in relation to the perforations. For example "centred top" means it is closer to the top perforation (or may even be cut by it) then the bottom, whilst "centred south-east" (SE) indicates the design is down to the right in the bottom right-hand corner. In some issues where centring is generally poor a well centred stamp will command a premium, in other issues where good centring is the norm the poorly centred specimen may be virtually worthless (but see *freak perforations*).

Ceres. 1) The Roman goddess of corn whose head, garlanded with ears of corn representing the earth's fertility, appears on early French stamps, and on later issues of France, Portugal and other countries. 2) A well known catalogue of the stamps of France and French colonies published by the company of the same name in Paris.

Certificate. Issued by members of a panel of experts (or expert committee) to warrant the genuiness or otherwise of a stamp or cover. In Great Britain both the Royal Society and the British Philatelic Association issue certificates as do one or two dealers. A certificate of genuineness almost certainly means that the value of a rare or expensive item is enhanced and the chances of selling improved.

Chalk Surfaced Paper, Chalky (C). A paper which has been coated with a chalky solution which has the effect of tying the cancellation to the stamp. Thus it cannot be removed without damaging the design of the stamp. A simple test for chalk surfaced paper is to rub the surface with a silver object, whereupon a "pencil line" is produced. Always do this in a part of the design where it will not be noticeable.

Chalon Head. Descriptive of any stamp bearing the full face portrait of Queen Victoria taken from Alfred Edward Chalon's painting of her in coronation robes. It was used on many issues printed by Perkins, Bacon for Bahamas, Natal, New Zealand, Queensland and Tasmania as well as the famous *Twelvepenny Black of Canada*.

Chambon Perforation. A type of comb perforation which perforates one complete stamp and half of two sides of the two adjacent stamps. The comb then moves two stamp widths and the next pass completes the half perforated stamp plus a complete stamp and another half. Where the registration is not exact a thicker or thinner tooth will be left at the centre of each side.

Charity Stamp. A stamp issued to raise funds in support of a charity, (vast numbers are not postage stamps). A postage stamp so issued will normally show a surcharge, either printed as part of the design or overprinted upon it, to show how much of the cost of the stamp is passed to the charity (after expenses). Many countries issue or have issued charity stamps. Some such as the Swiss "Pro Juventute" and New Zealand "Health" appear every year, others only in particular circumstances, such as hurricane or flood relief funds.

Check Letters. The early stamps issued in Great Britain had letters in the bottom two corners (and later all four corners). They were intended to hamper forgery but now enable collectors to build up complete reconstructions of the original sheets. The lettering in the bottom left corner ran from A in the top row, B in the second row etc., and in the bottom right corner from A in the first column, B in the second column etc. Thus the stamp in the top left corner of the sheet was lettered AA whilst the adjoining stamp to its right was lettered AB as compared with the adjoining stamp below it which was lettered BA. These letter combinations are the ones in the bottom corners of the stamps, the letters in the top corner were the same but in reverse order. Thus stamp AF would have letters FA at the top. The knowledge of where the gutter margins occurred in relation to the various letter combinations is an important guide to detecting cut down *wing margins* on later surface printed issues.

Cherry Blossom. A popular name for the second issue of Japanese stamps issued in August 1872. They are so called because of the small flower shown in the corners.

Chop. Another name for a security overprint made by a commercial company.

Christmas Stamp. Many countries issue special Christmas stamps each year for use on Christmas mail. The designs generally reflect either religious or festive scenes appropriate to the season.

Cinderella. Stamps not issued by the official Post Office organisation for postage although some may nevertheless have some local postal use. Largely neglected by most collectors, cinderella stamps include fiscals, telegraphs, railway and airway letter and parcel stamps, exhibition and commemorative labels and vignettes, Christmas seals etc. etc.

Circular Date Stamp (CDS). A type of cancel having the date enclosed in a circle which may also show the town and country name, the time of posting etc. One half of a *duplex cancel* is generally a circular date stamp and it is very often a part of a modern machine cancel. Generally a stamp having a CDS is preferred by collectors of used stamps to most other types of cancel or obliterator.

Classics. The term usually refers to the first or very early stamps issued up to about 1870 but some more recent issues such as the 1948 Silver Wedding series have become modern classics. It implies stamps of good design with a steadily appreciating value which have remained popular with collectors irrespective of passing fads and fancies (see also *Primitives*).

Clean Cut. Perforations in which the holes have been cleanly cut and the paper removed (see *Rough perforations*).

Cleaned. Descriptive of a stamp which has been treated

chemically, indicating that a fiscal or other cancel has been removed from it, by bleach or other agent, leaving the stamp in apparently pristine condition.

Cleaned Plate. With continued use a printing plate may become clogged with ink, especially in areas of fine detail. The impressions produced are of poor quality. After cleaning the plate the impressions revert to a quality similar to that of the first printings from the plate when new, in which all the details are in sharp relief.

Cliché. A stereotype or electrotype plate. Usually used in the form "substituted cliché" indicating that one impression of the original plate has become damaged and has been completely replaced by the new one.

Club. Many collectors belong to local philatelic societies or clubs. These meet regularly and provide a social background to collecting and a venue for displays by collectors to other collectors, bourses etc. There are also clubs which relate to specific countries or collecting interests though with their more scattered memberships the meetings tend to be less frequent. Members are very often kept in touch with each other by newsletters and magazines. Details of local philatelic societies are usually available at local public libraries.

Coated. A description of any paper with a special coating, e.g. chalk-surfaced or glazed papers. The principle reason for coating is to prevent the removal of the postmark without at the same time removing the design.

Coil. A stamp issued in a roll principally for use in stamp vending machines. Sometimes the rolls are printed continuously, sometimes they are made up from ordinary sheets so that there is a coil join at regular intervals where the selvedge occurs. Very often coil stamps are imperforate on two sides, only being perforated across the roll.

Coil Leader. A printed band which seals the roll of stamps on which is printed details of the content of the coil such as the quantity, and the face value and other information. They are also used to help thread the loose end of the coil through the mechanism of the machine.

Coil Perforation. Some stamps are produced with specially enlarged perforation holes to make separation easier. These are normally only identifiable when the stamps are still in pairs (see also *Schermack perforation*).

College Stamp. Between 1871 and 1886 both Oxford and Cambridge Universities issued stamps for use on letters carried by their own messenger services. They are *Locals* since they were not valid in the postal service proper.

Collotype. A method of printing used by a number of forgers to produce plausible forgeries.

Colour Change. Indicates that the stamp is printed in a colour different from that in which it was first issued. This may have been to conform with *UPU colour regulations* following a change in postal rates or because the first colour or combination proved to be unsatisfactory for some reason.

Colour Changeling. Name given to a stamp whose colour has been altered, usually by the action of light or water, subsequent to printing.

Colour Proof. Similar to a *colour trial* except that it is taken in the colour in which the stamp is to be printed. If satisfactory, it enables the final "go-ahead to print" instruction to be given to the printer.

Colour Shift. Caused in multiple colour printing when one of the colour cylinders does not line up correctly with the others, sometimes producing startling results on the printed stamp. Mostly ignored by philatelists unless the shift is of a particularly dramatic nature when it may command a premium.

Colour Trial. A stamp printed to judge colour quality and appearance to enable a final decision on the colour to be used to be made.

Coloured Paper. Many countries have issued stamps printed on coloured or tinted paper usually to help enable identification of different stamp values more easily. The paper may be either coloured throughout at manufacture stage or coloured on one surface only.

Column. A vertical line of stamps in the sheet identified by numbering from the left.

Comb Perforation. The perforation pins when viewed from above are arranged in the form of a comb and perforate three sides of each stamp in the row at the same time. The next beat perforates the fourth side (which is also the first side of the next row of stamps). Stamps perforated on a comb machine are easily recognised since the corner holes are symmetrical and in register (see *line perforation, chambon perforation*).

Combination Cover. A cover which bears stamps of two or more countries in order to pay the postage along the route followed.

Commemorative. Literally a stamp or cover issued to commemorate a special event either past or present, sometimes as part of an *omnibus issue* . Colloquially, any stamp used for normal postage purposes which is not a *definitive* which is on sale for a restricted period of time and which may form part of a small set related by theme or topic. Many so called commemoratives are more correctly called *special issues* .

Commonwealth. 1) Refers to the countries comprising the British Commonwealth at various times, which form a popular collecting area even though some of those countries are no longer members. 2) Refers to the catalogue published by *Bridger and Kaye* which details stamps and their varieties issued by the countries comprising the British Commonwealth.

Composite Cards. The name given to picture postcards where a number of cards are required in order to make up the complete design. Usually three to twelve cards make up a composite set.

Composite Sheet. Different values printed in the same sheet so that by cutting, booklet panes or miniature sheets may be obtained.

Compound Envelope (or Card). Official postal stationery which has more than one printed or embossed stamp.

Compound Perforation. A term to indicate a stamp has two or more different perforations on its sides. Stamps very often have different guage perforations at top and bottom compared with those at the sides. This is to help prevent the sheet from splitting unnecessarily without at the same time making it difficult for the post office clerk to separate stamps cleanly when required.

Condition. The state of the stamp upon which its value may be judged. When judging condition the following will all be considered: colour; centring; cancellation (if it is used); gum if it is mint; whether it is torn, creased or otherwise damaged; whether the perforations are sound; if it is imperforate whether it has margins; whether there are any stains, foxing, rust spots or other marks or discolouration etc. etc. Degrees of condition in general use in descending order are as follows for used stamps: superb; very fine; good; average; poor. For mint stamps: unmounted mint (unhinged mint or mint, never hinged); lightly mounted mint; mint; full original gum; part original gum (see also *Mint, Unused, Used*).

Condominium. Inscription which shows that the country concerned was administered by two external powers. In modern times the term can only be correctly applied to the Sudan (Britain and Egypt) and the New Hebrides (Britain and France).

Connoisseur. A shortened reference to the "Connoisseur Catalogue of Machin Printings" which is perhaps the most comprehensive listing of these issues with details of all the different heads, papers and varieties etc.

Control Marks. 1) Marks or lines used by printers in order to ensure correct registration of colours when printing. 2) Marks or lines used by printers to identify a particular plate not otherwise numbered. 3) Marks added to printed stamps in order to control their use, or to restrict the use of unoverprinted stamps following a major theft or the discovery of a major forgery operation.

Control Number. Letters and numbers printed in the margin of Great Britain stamps so that the particular printing can be identified (see also *Plate number, Millésime*).

Copy. 1) A facsimile or imitation. 2) A single specimen or stamp usually further described as in the expressions "a fine copy" or "a damaged copy".

Cork Cancel. Cancellation produced by using a cork cut with a design on the flat surface. Very prevalent in Canada and the

USA in the nineteenth century but not used very much elsewhere. They were used by local postmasters to cancel stamps when they had not been issued with any official cancellor. Some cork cancellors were actually made of wood or rubber. There are many designs and they form a fascinating area of study.

Corner Block. Describes a block of stamps from the corner of the sheet and therefore having sheet margins on two sides.

Corner Letters. See *check letters*.

Cotton Reels. A popular name given to the stamps issued in British Guiana in 1850–1 since they resembled the labels stuck on the ends of reels of sewing cotton sold in shops.

Cover. Usually an envelope which has carried its contents through the postal system and which bears evidence of this fact in the form of adhesive stamps and postmarks, cancellations.

Cracked Plate. A fault occurring on the printing plate, perhaps by misuse, which is evident on the printed stamp by coloured or colourless lines corresponding to the crack. Philatelists are able to use these as plating guides.

Crash Cover. A cover bearing a *cachet* or other indication that it has been retrieved from a crashed aeroplane (see *wreck cover*).

Creased Transfer. The paper plate has been creased or otherwise distorted when placed on the litho plate during plate making. The effect shows as a distorted area on the printed stamp.

Cross. A widely used symbol in stamp design, also for watermarks and cancellations. Also as the *St Andrew's Cross* to prevent blank stamp labels being used by forgers.

Crown. A crown features in many stamp designs and watermarks of countries which have or have had a monarchy. The term crown is usually further classified according to size or shape. Some such as the Tudor crown or St Edward's crown are named after the crowns they were intended to represent. Many crown watermarks also incorporate letters, sometimes attached to the top or bottom of the crown. These may either be the *royal cypher* or represent the name of the country, for example

"NSW" for New South Wales; or the supplying agent, for example "CA" for the Crown Agents.

Crown Agents (CA). A large government-sponsored organisation responsible among other things for the production and distribution or postage stamps for many of the Crown Colonies and members of the British Commonwealth.

Crown CA. A watermark comprising a crown above the block capital letters "CA" used by the Crown Agents during the period 1883–1905. In 1904 a multiple version was introduced which remained in use until it too was superceded by *Multiple Script CA watermark* in the 1920s.

Crown CC. A watermark comprising a crown above the block letters CC used by the Crown Agents until about 1885.

Crown Watermark. Several crown watermarks using varying patterns of crown have been used both for the Great Britain stamps and in other countries also. These generally fall into the following categories: small crown, large crown or multiple crown. Many crown watermarks incorporate a letter either above or below the crown in either single or multiple format. Sometimes the crown may be identifiable as a particular crown such as the Imperial crown, the Tudor crown etc. All crown watermarks are usually clearly illustrated in the appropriate catalogues or handbooks.

Cut-Out. The part of official stationery bearing the printed or embossed stamp which has been cut from the card or envelope. Such cut-outs, providing they have not previously been cancelled, are valid for postage if stuck on postal items. Many cut-outs find their way into stamp albums because of collectors' mistaken beliefs that they are rare stamps or non-catalogued printings etc. Some catalogues, notably in the USA, quote prices for them but generally speaking postal stationery is usually better collected intact.

Cut Square. A term used to describe an imperforate stamp with an irregular shaped design, or more than four sides in a regular design, which has been cut to a four sided shape around the design. For example an octagonal stamp would be cut square if it had four imperforate sides compared with the eight sides it would have had if it had been cut following the design of the stamp. Cut square stamps are more sought after by collectors and more valuable than copies of the same stamp which have been cut to shape.

Cut To Shape. Imperforate stamp with an irregular design or design with more than four sides whose margins have been cut to follow the outer frame of the design. Usually worth less than cut square copies of the same stamp.

Cylinder. Modern printing presses have the printing plates in cylindrical form as opposed to flat bed. There is one for each colour.

Cylinder Number. Each cylinder plate is allocated a number. Since each colour requires its own cylinder, it follows that each colour has its own cylinder number. In multi-colour printing the number on each cylinder may be the same, so a further letter is added to help in identification. The cylinder number is usually engraved on the plate and is thus printed in the margin of each sheet of stamps. Cylinder numbers may be followed by a dot, the presence or absence of which indicates from which side, left or right, of the cylinder that particular sheet was printed.

Cylinder Number Block. A block of stamps with the margin on which the cylinder numbers are printed still attached.

Dandy Roller. A roller usually made of wire gauze beneath which pulp passes when paper is made and which imparts the texture and watermark (if any) to the paper. The watermark is produced by metal or wire designs which are incorporated into the dandy roller and slightly raised from it. The paper where the watermark occurs is therefore slightly thinner and hence the watermark shows up when the paper is viewed with a light behind it.

Date Stamp. Any postal marking which contains a date. It may either be a handstamp or part of a machine cancel.

Dealer. Anyone who buys and sells stamps for a profit. This may be either at a shop, or at a stamp fair or bourse, or through the post by means of approvals or advertising.

Deckle Edged. The rough edge of handmade paper made in a deckle or frame. This sometimes forms the edge of a stamp printed on such paper especially if the stamp is imperforate or has been *harrow perforated*.

Definitives. The main issues intended to provide for the postal needs of a country for an indefinite period of time and which provide a full range of face values. This contrasts with *commemoratives* or special issues which have a limited on-sale period and cover a restricted range of face values.

Deferential Postmark. A postmark designed in such a way that, whilst the stamp is cancelled, the portrait (usually the reigning monarch) is not defaced. The effect was very often like an ornamental mirror with the frame provided by the postmark, the reflection being the face of the stamp.

De La Rue (DLR). Thomas De La Rue and Co. Ltd, one of the major British stamp printers.

Delacryl. A form of multicoloured litho printing used by De La Rue and Co. Ltd.

Deltiologist. A picture postcard collector.

Demonetised. Any issue of stamps no longer valid for their original purpose. For example Great Britain's pre-decimal stamps became demonetised after the introduction of decimal currency and stamps.

Designer. The person who designs the stamps and provides the final artwork from which the printing plates are derived.

Detector. A device for assisting the philatelist in the detection and identification of watermarks either by the use of light and filters, or spirit such as benzine or lighter fuel.

Dickinson Paper. Named after its inventor, it is a paper which has long silk threads in it. It was used for some early issues of Great Britain, German States and Switzerland as well as the famous *Mulready Envelopes*.

Die. The piece of metal on which the design of the stamp is first engraved is often called the master or mother die. After hardening it is used either directly or via a transfer roller to reproduce identical impressions on the plate from which the stamp will be printed. The original die is termed Die I. Any later versions will be numbered in sequence Die II, Die III etc. and stamps printed from them are usually distinguishable from the originals by small differences in the engraving.

Die Proof. A single impression taken from the master die usually in black on white card. This will be closely examined to ensure that the die has been engraved correctly. If alterations are necessary further die proofs will be taken until perfection is achieved. The die will then be authorised for use in creating the printing plates.

Discount Postage. Mint postage stamps sold at below face value usually to encourage a greater use of the postal services.

Disinfected Mail. Mail which has been treated to prevent infection from spreading. Various methods were used such as dipping the letter in vinegar, holding the letter over a brazier in a fumigating box etc. Sometimes special postal markings were applied to indicate that disinfection had taken place. Sometimes the marks of the tongs (used to hold the letters over the brazier) or a chisel cut are the only evidence.

Divided Back. Picture postcards published after 1897, when the message and the address were allowed to be written on the same side. This side showed a division across the centre usually with an indication that the stamp and address were to go on the right side and the message to be written on the left.

Dockwra. William Dockwra, a London merchant, set up a private post in the city in 1680. It was closed down following legal action by the General Post Office, through the Duke of York, in 1682. Letters carried by the post may have two postmarks, one to indicate payment has been made and the other the time of despatch. Letters carried by the service are known as Dockwras whilst later letters carried after the Post Office had set up its own service are termed Government Dockwras and later still the London District Post.

Doctor Blade. A steel blade on the printing press which removes surplus ink from the printing surface of the photogravure cylinder. When it does not function correctly it gives rise to lines or streaks of colour on the printed stamp known as doctor blade flaws. These are non-constant varieties since the malfunction, usually because of the intrusion of a bit of grit or other substance, is generally only of a temporary nature.

Dominical Label. Detached *tab* attached to certain Belgian stamps which if not torn off requested that the letter should not be delivered on a Sunday.

Dot and No-Dot. A term used to indicate from which side of a single cylinder a particular pane or sheet has been printed. The cylinder numbers will be the same on each pane so a dot is added after the cylinder number on the right hand pane, thus no-dot equals left pane, dot equals right.

Dotted Circle. A particular type of *circular date stamp* in which the outer circle or frame line consist of a series of dots or dashes instead of a continuous line.

Double Letter. On the early stamps of Great Britain letters were added to the printing plate by use of a hammer and hand punch. It was necessary to use several blows of the hammer to ensure a deep enough impression. If the bit of the punch moved between the blows, the resulting print from the plate showed an irregularity in that particular letter, generally described as a double letter.

Double Paper. Paper made up of two different layers, usually used in the belief that any attempt to remove the cancellation would also cause the different papers to come apart. It occasionally occurs where paper on the roll has been joined, resulting in a double thickness.

Double Printing. Either part or the whole of the image appears twice. 1) May be intentional as in the case of the twenty-öre Swedish stamp of 1876 which was first printed in a yellow colour which faded badly. The sheets were printed again in a different colour and where the registration did not coincide the double printing was visible. 2) May be accidental, caused by vibration in the printing press or by a sheet being fed through twice or some other malfunction. Double printing is probably commonest on overprints with two and sometimes three appearing on one stamp. 3) Doubling may also be caused by *re-entry* of the plate in which case the doubling is not due to the printing and will show on every copy of that stamp in the position on the sheet.

Downey Heads. Refers to the first halfpenny and penny George V stamps of Great Britain which used a three-quarter profile of the king's head based on a photograph by W & D Downey.

Dragons. A popular name for the first issue of Japanese stamps in 1871 which showed a dragon on either side of the value in the centre panel.

Dropped Letter. Usually applied to a letter (or character) which has been dropped or ejected from the forme in which it was held. This results in it being missing from the inscription on that stamp on sheets printed after it happened. Sometimes descriptive of a letter which is out of alignment.

Dry Print. A stamp image or overprint which shows hardly any ink due to an inking deficiency in the printing.

Duck Stamps. Hunting permit stamps of the USA so called because most issues feature some species of duck or other water bird in the design.

Due. Postage label used to show that postage due is to be or was paid on delivery as the item was insufficiently prepaid.

Dumb Cancellation. A cancellation which has no identifying inscription. They take several forms including black bars, concentric rings (or target cancels) wavy lines etc.

Dumb Stamp. A stamp which omits the country's name from the design. In this respect all stamps of Great Britain are dumb, but there are also examples from other countries such as the USA and Austria. Also stamps which omit the value but which are sold for particular amounts usually corresponding with current postal rates.

Duplex Cancellation. A handstamp formed of two adjacent parts, a date stamp to fall on the cover, and an obliterator, usually of bars, to cancel the stamp. There are many different variations and many countries used them. Apart from some small US post offices they have not been in general use since before World War I.

Duty Plate. In multi-plate stamps, the plate used to print the postal duty or face value is called the duty plate. Where the design for each value is the same, one *key plate* or *head plate* may be used for all values, but a different duty plate will be required to print each different face value.

Duty Stamp. A stamp used to collect duty, i.e. a postage stamp collects postal duty, a revenue or fiscal may collect stamp duty and other taxes. Postage due labels are frequently used to collect import duty on goods being imported via the postal service.

Eagles. A popular name for the 1864 issues of Mexico which showed an eagle trampling a snake under foot. Also applied to the 1845 and 1847–9 issues of Geneva.

Electrotyping. A means of copying a design impressed in a mould, usually wax, by electrolysis. A layer of copper is built up on the design and when suitably strengthened and hardened this will become the printing plate. It has been widely used in stamp printing since about 1850.

Elizabethan. Usually a reference to the Stanley Gibbons catalogue "Specialised Listing of British Commonwealth Elizabethan Stamps" covering all the issues of the reign of Queen Elizabeth II.

Embossing. A means of creating an impression by distorting the paper and leaving the design on the raised surface of the paper. Sometimes the embossed area is also printed in colour but usually it remains colourless. Many embossed stamps tend to split at the place where the embossing joins the normal surface which is the weakest part. Such damage reduces the value of these stamps considerably. Stamps having sharp clear embossing command a premium.

En Épargne. In this form of engraving the unwanted portions of the design are removed leaving the areas which will appear as the printed lines of the design untouched. The opposite of *intaglio*, also known as surface printing.

Enamelled Paper. A rather brittle paper with a surface coating of a solution of zinc white and glue.

End Delivery. Roll stamps joined at the narrowest side for use in automatic vending machines.

Endorsement. Printing on the back of a stamp, almost always for security reasons. It may take the form of numerals, pseudo watermarks or even a company's name or initials. Also known as underprints or backprints.

Engine Turning. A means of engraving symmetrical patterns mechanically by the use of a geometric lathe called the improved rose engine. Many stamps are found with this and it was used on both the Penny Black and Twopenny Blue as long ago as 1840.

Engraving. See *Line Engraving*.

Entire. Originally a single sheet on which the letter was written on one side and which when folded and sealed had the address and postal markings applied to the outside. Now extended to include covers with stamps attached and containing the original letter or contents etc.

Envelope. The usual outer cover in which a letter is inserted for transmission through the post. Envelopes are also sold by the postal authorities bearing the impressed postage stamp, and therefore requiring no further adhesives unless the minimum weight steps are exceeded.

Envelope Cut Squares. The American equivalent of *cut-outs*.

Epaulettes. Popular name for the first Belgium issues of 1849 in which King Leopold I was shown wearing a uniform with epaulettes on the shoulders. They were much criticised and were replaced by the *medallion* issues a few months later.

Erased. A term used to indicate that a portion of the design or overprint has been deliberately removed, usually by erasing it from the printing plate.

Error. Specifically a stamp which has something abnormal as compared with a normal stamp of the same design or issue. 1) Colour. Stamps printed in the wrong colour. 2) Design. Stamps where an error occurs in the design such as a misspelt name, an incorrect accent or an upside-down flag. 3) Paper. Stamps printed on the wrong paper either by mistake or perhaps in an emergency when the usual paper was not available. 4) Perforation. Stamps perforated at the wrong gauge or in the wrong place in relation to the margin, or not perforated on one or more sides when they should have been. 5) Printing. Stamps with double printing, inverted printing etc. caused by wrong paper feeding. 6) Plate. Stamps with errors caused by wrong plate construction, for example an inverted centre or frame. 7) Watermark. Stamps printed on the wrong paper very often have the wrong watermark particularly if the watermark is a numeral relating to the face value of the stamp. Another error occurs when part of the watermark design on the *dandy roll* is itself incorrect. Watermarks normally appear upright and readable when viewed from the front. However, some stamps are printed normally with the watermark sideways or inverted. Errors occur when the paper is fed in incorrectly and the watermark appears in a different way from stamps printed normally.

Estimate. Given by auctioneers as their opinion of the value of a particular lot in an auction and a particularly useful guide to postal bidders. Some auctioneers appear to estimate low in order to attract as many bids and room bidders as possible even though many will be disappointed. Others quote catalogue price, only showing an estimate when the condition of the item means that the catalogue price is not a fair guide to its value. Collectors too will have their opinion as to the value of a lot and will bid accordingly. Since opinions differ, and bidders' priorities also, the knockdown price may differ considerably from the estimate.

Etching. A means of transferring a design into the surface of a metal plate by the use of an acid. Etching can also be done manually or by photo mechanical means.

Ethnic. A term used by thematic and picture postcard collectors to indicate an item illustrating the inhabitants of a country in their national costumes or performing characteristic activities.

Etiquette. The name given to items such as airmail, recorded delivery, express or registration labels and stickers.

Europa. Stamps issued by certain European countries commemorate the annual European Postal and Telecommunications Conference (CEPT). Very often a common design is used by most countries, presumably to promote the image of a united Europe.

Exchange Club. A club in which stamps belonging to members are circulated to other members for the purpose of buying and selling.

Exhibition Labels. Special labels designed to publicise exhibitions for use on letters and correspondence but having no postal validity. Do not confuse them with special exhibition commemorative stamps issued by postal authorities.

Expedition Stamps. Stamps issued for use by members of scientific or military expeditions. They are very often normal issues overprinted for the purpose. Many expeditions utilise normal issues but their letters bear suitable *cachets* including censor or other marks to indicate their connection with the expedition.

Expertisation. The examination of a stamp by a recognised expert (or committee of experts) in order to establish or deny its authenticity. A certificate or other endorsement may be given.

Express. A faster method of postal delivery than the normal service and costing more. Special express stamps have been issued by many countries and these fall into letter, airmail, newspaper, parcel and even personal categories. Many countries merely use the normal postage stamp to collect the extra fee and put a suitable *etiquette* or postmark on the item to be carried.

Extension Hole. A single perforation hole in the margin of a sheet of stamps as an extention to the line of perforation between the stamps.

Fabs. Special postcards which had a square of silk with a design on it attached. They were advertisements for Sharpe's of Bradford. The silk square could be used for patchwork etc.

Face or Face Value. The denomination or monetary value for which the stamp is sold over the post office counter and which is normally indicated on the stamp. In the case of a charity stamp it is the sum of the postage and fund amounts which are shown.

Facsimile. A printed copy in similar colour of an issued stamp. Unlike a *forgery* it is not intended to deceive or defraud and very often incorporates the word facsimile in the stamp.

Faded. All printing inks and papers fade if left for prolonged periods in sunlight or soaked too long in water. Bleach solutions used to clean stamps also cause colours to fade. Faded stamps are worth far less than stamps with good original colour.

Fake. A stamp which has been altered in some way in order to make it appear as something it is not. Usually done to defraud the collector (as opposed to the *forgery* which is intended to defraud the Post Office) it may fall into any one of the following categories: 1) Repaired stamps where damage or defects such as thins and tears are skilfully hidden. 2) Perforated stamps made to appear imperforate by trimming the edge, particularly on marginal examples where the margins themselves are already imperforate. 3) Reperforating *wing margin* stamps to normal size or otherwise repairing perforations. 4) Regumming the backs of apparently unused copies (very often cleaned copies from which fiscal cancellations have been removed) to make them appear mint. 5) Adding bogus or forged postmarks to mint stamps when they are much rarer in their used condition. 6) Adding bogus or forged overprints with or without errors. 7) Simulating watermarks by use of oil and rubber stamps, etc. etc. Collectors should always examine stamps very carefully and if in doubt consult a reputable dealer or acknowledged expert.

Fancy Cancel. Term used to describe some of the more exotic cancellations which appear on stamps. To a certain extent synonymous with *Cork cancel*.

Fantail. Popular name for a marginal copy of a perforated stamp which is imperforate between the design and the margin, quite common on sheets perforated using a *harrow perforator*.

Field Post Office (FPO). An Army post office set up for handling *soldiers' mail* when on active service. The postmarks on such mail merely show the inscription Field Post Office or FPO and the number with no indication of the location of that post office.

File Crease. A crease usually in a cover or entire, very often in addition to the original folds, due to the item having been kept folded for a period of time.

Fine (F). Qualifies the condition of a stamp or philatelic item indicating that it is sound and desirable and of above average condition.

First Day Cover (FDC). A cover bearing a date stamp tying the stamps and showing the date as the first day of issue of the stamp. Very often a special circular date stamp is used and specially illustrated covers are produced using similar themes to the stamps. These covers may be produced either by the Post Office or by private companies. In Britain all FDCs must pass through the post although some countries will permit the handstamping of covers at the post office for the collector to take away. The abbreviation FDC will normally indicate an illustrated or official FDC with the special cancel for issues where these were available. However, envelopes used in the regular post on the first day of issue are also first day covers but bear an ordinary CDS. Before special cancels and envelopes were introduced all first day covers appear as normal postal items with only the date of the CDS to confirm the first day status.

First Flight Cover. This is a souvenir cover carried on the inaugural flight over a new airmail route, or the introduction of a new type of aircraft onto an existing route or some other specific change or innovation. Earlier items very often carry a special *cachet*, whilst more recently special printed envelopes (similar to FDCs) have been provided. In some cases specially overprinted stamps and/or cancellations have been used.

Fiscal. 1) A stamp specially used for the collection of revenues or taxes of a non-postal nature. Some stamps are valid for both postal and fiscal purposes in which case: 2) A cancel on a stamp indicating it has been used fiscally (i.e. to collect revenues or taxes) and not postally. Generally fiscal cancels are readily recognisable, usually in purple or red. (Postal cancellations are usually but not always in black.) Many show the name of the company, bank or other institution and are generally on a larger scale than postal cancellations. In the absence of a suitable cancellor many fiscal cancellations may be simple *pen cancels* with a signature and date or other wording. Not all pen cancels are fiscal however. A fiscal cancel on a posage stamp reduces its value. 3) Fiscal stamps which have been authorised on occasions for postal use can legitimately form part of a postage stamp collection. These must of course be collected either in mint condition or with clear and genuine postal cancels. Fiscal stamps used on covers sell at a premium above a loose copy of the same stamp.

Flag Cancel. Some machine cancellors had part of the design in the form of a flag. They were very popular in the period 1880–1920 in Canada and USA, and also some other countries. They are best collected on cover if possible or at the very least a complete strike on a piece with full CDS showing the town of origin and date.

Flat Plate. A printing plate which is flat, and used in flat bed printing. Although the same design may be printed using flat or curved plates (cylinders) produced from the same master die, there will be sufficient difference in the size of the printed impression for each printing to be identifiable.

Flaw. An imperfection in the design of the printed stamp caused by some damage or foreign body affecting the printing plate. If it is damaged then all sheets printed from that plate will show a stamp or stamps with the same flaw in the same position. This is known as a constant flaw and may achieve catalogue status as a variety. If it is caused by damage it may become progressively more pronounced as printing proceeds giving rise to various states or further varieties. A foreign body adhering to the plate will also cause a flaw but since at some stage it is likely to be dislodged or moved or simply cleaned off this is termed a non-constant flaw and whilst interesting in itself will be unlikely to achieve catalogue status.

Flong. A papier mâché sheet sometimes used to make a mould of a design or plate. When dry it will be used to take a cast in metal of the design or plate which is being copied.

Flown Cover. A cover which had been carried on an airmail route and bears suitable cancellations or *cachets* confirming the fact.

Fluorescence. Ultra violet light causes many printing inks to fluoresce, thus the presence or absence of fluorescence may be used in several ways: 1) To reveal forged or repaired stamps. 2) To identify different printings of the same stamp. 3) To aid mechanical letter handling in Post Office sorting offices.

Fly Speck. See *Variety*.

Forerunners. Term used to describe stamps in use in a country prior to stamps of that country becoming available. Thus stamps of the Australian States (New South Wales, Queensland etc.) are forerunners to Commonwealth of Australia issues, whilst the stamps of British Honduras are forerunners to the stamps of Belize even though only the name changed. Similarly stamps of India used in Pakistan prior to the issue of Pakistan stamps would be forerunners whilst the stamps of Pakistan used in Bangladesh prior to the establishment of that country would themselves be forerunners as would the Indian stamps used earlier.

Forgery. A close copy of a stamp intended to deceive with fraudulent intent. A philatelic forgery would be produced, after a stamp has ceased to be available from the Post Office, with the intent of defrauding collectors into believing it genuine (and therefore valuable) since these forgeries were confined in the main to rare and valuable stamps (see *Fake*). A postal forgery was intended to defraud the postal authorities either by selling to the public for postal use, or being used by the forger himself to defraud an employer (see *Stock Exchange forgery*).

Sometimes forged overprints or cancellations were applied to genuine stamps and this fact should be noted in any description of such stamps by use of wording such as "stamp genuine but forged overprint". Some forgeries, particularly the postal ones, are worth more than the genuine stamps but these are the exception rather than the rule and most collectors will not pay more than a nominal amount for a forgery (see *Propaganda*).

Format. Describes the shape and direction of a stamp design. Portrait or vertical indicates it is higher than it is wide; landscape or horizontal that it is wider than it is high. Other formats include round, diamond, triangular and even irregular or free form.

Foxed, foxing. The paper stamps are printed on is sometimes attacked by a fungus which shows as brown spots and gradually eats away the paper. It usually occurs in inadequate storage conditions, and it can be transmitted from stamp to stamp via the album page. It can be arrested by the use of some chemicals and proprietary preparations but these are only recommended for used stamps. It is also known as rust or rusting, and sometimes confused with *toning* which is more often the result of gum discolouration.

Fractional Stamps. A term sometimes used to describe stamps designed to be cut into halves or quarters, the smaller piece retaining postal validity for the half or quarter value of the original stamp. Official bisects are also sometimes described in this way. The small parts of the stamp are also known as splits.

Frame. The printed outer edge or border of a stamp or *vignette*.

Frank. 1) A mark, signature or other device which indicates that the item to which it is applied may be carried through the post free of charge. 2) A handstamp or machine cancel indicating that postage has been prepaid and therefore no further charge is to be made. Hence modern franking machines where payment in advance allows mail to be franked until the meter recording the amount of money unused registers zero.

Freak Perforations. These indicate that the perforations are totally out of register with the stamp impression either by misalignment of the sheet or by the sheet being folded in some way when it was perforated.

Free Form, Free Shape. A stamp printed in an irregular shape, used extensively by Sierra Leone and Tonga, and in most cases self-adhesive.

Fresh. A term used by dealers and auctioneers to indicate that a stamp still retains the quality of having just been printed, with fine original colour and paper showing no signs of fading or discolouration.

Front. The front or address side of a cover, but usually still retaining the adhesive or postal markings.

FRPSL. Abbreviation for Fellow of the Royal Philatelic Society of London.

Fugitive. Description of an ink which runs when it gets wet, used as a security device to prevent stamps being cleaned and re-used. A stamp with fugitive ink on which the colour has run (possibly when removed from the original envelope) is of little value when compared with one still maintaining its true colour.

Galvanotype. Named after the famous pioneer scientist of electricity, Luigi Galvani. The process is more usually known as *electrotype*.

Gauge. A means of defining the difference between perforations (and *roulettes*). These are gauged by counting the number of holes occurring in a two-centimetre length. A perforation gauge is a specially ruled instrument to make the measurement of the perforations on a stamp easier for the collector. Many different makes are available, perhaps the best and most accurate being the Stanley Gibbons Instanta.

Another type of gauge, the Thirkell Position Finder, uses a grid marking to define the position of flaws on a stamp.

Yet another gauge, the Fisher Alphabet Comparator, shows the complete different alphabets of the corner letters on early Great Britain stamps thus assisting in plate identification.

General Issues. A description used in some catalogues for *definitive* stamps, where such issues are shown separately from special issues such as airmails, charities and express delivery stamps etc.

General Letter Office. The former name of the British Post Office, originally established in 1660 by an Act of Parliament.

Gladstone Roulette. Also known as the Treasury Roulette, since it was applied unofficially to the imperforate stamps used by the Treasury during Gladstone's term as Chancellor of the Exchequer 1850–4 (see *Roulette*).

Glass. A shortened name for a magnifying glass used by philatelists for studying the details of a stamp (see *Magnifiers*).

Glassine. A special type of see-through or semi see-through paper used for making small packets for housing stamps and also for the strips on the pages of some stock books.

Glazed Paper. A paper with a highly glossed surface achieved by super calendering but which has no other coating added. Also known as glacé paper (see *Chalk or Enamelled paper*).

Goldbeater's Skin. See *Resin paper*.

Government Parcels. In 1883 parcels sent on government service in the United Kingdom were required to pay a special rate: until then they had been free. Normal stamps corresponding to the rates were overprinted for use on such parcels. The special rates were altered several times and ceased altogether in 1904.

Grand Consommation Paper. A rather poor quality grey *granite paper* used in France as emergency supplies for some stamps at the end of World War I. The initials GC appear in the margin and it is sometimes known as GC paper.

Granite Paper. Paper in which both bleached and unbleached fibres are combined in the manufacture. The unbleached fibres show at the surface as tiny coloured strands.

Graphite. An electricity-conducting substance used experimentally on Great Britain stamps in connection with the automatic letter facing machines used in sorting offices. It was printed as one or two lines on the back of the stamp underneath the glue. It was later superceded by *Phosphor*.

Gravure. Another name for *photogravure* and similar printing processes operated under various trade names.

Green Cross Labels. Special green labels issued on a restricted basis to servicemen in Malta during World War II, for use by their families on letters to the island. Items bearing green cross labels were given priority on the limited airmail space on direct flights between the United Kingdom and Malta. Other mail was sent via the Cape of Good Hope and therefore took much longer.

Grid. The name given to cancellation of criss-cross lines very often found on the earlier stamps of USA and France. They are found in either circular, square or lozenge shapes.

Grill. 1) A security device by which the surface of a stamp is broken by criss-cross or dotted embossing thereby allowing the ink of the cancellation to penetrate thus preventing cleaning and re-use. 2) A means of treating paper before gumming in order to prevent it from curling after the gum has been applied. 3) The markings on an album page provided to allow easier and more accurate layout and writing up of a stamp collection (also known as quadrillé).

Gruss Aus. A description given to a particular type of picture postcard on which the words "Gruss aus" (which is German for "Greeting from") were printed on the picture side. They therefore formed part of the message, which on the earliest cards was also written on the picture side.

Guide Marks. 1) Lines or dots marked on a printing plate in order to aid the registration of the design by the plate maker. These are normally removed before the plate is used. They show as guide lines or guide dots on the printed stamps when the removal has not been properly completed and on many earlier stamps provide a means of allocating such stamps to a specific plate and position. 2) Lines or other marks printed by the individual colour cylinders in the sheet margins in order to help accurate registration of all colours. 3) Dots or crosses printed, or holes punched in the margins of sheets to help accurate registration of the perforating heads.

Gum. The adhesive applied to a stamp which enables the user to stick it to the envelope. Various types have been used, the most prevalent being gum arabic (sometimes known as gum acacia) which is normally shiny and slightly yellow due to impurities. In more recent years this has been superceded by polyvinyl alcohol gum (PVA) which is colourless and often has a colouring agent, such as dextrin, added so that the user can see that the gum is actually there.

The difference between gum on two otherwise identical stamps allows collectors to identify various printings.

The condition of the gum is important when assessing the value of a stamp. Many collectors collect *mint* stamps and will expect to pay less for a stamp on which the gum has been damaged or marked in any way. Older stamps are sometimes described as "full OG" or "part OG" indicating that they still have all or part of the original gum on the back. Other expressions such as "gum crazed" (where the surface of the gum resembles crazy paving or the paint surface of an old oil painting) or "gum crease" (where the gum has a crease mark which is not visible on the face of the stamp) are used by dealers to describe the gum condition of a stamp.

Gutter. The space between two stamps on the same sheet.

Gutter Margin. The margin between two panes of stamps. Sometimes these contain printing. The expression gutter pair indicates a pair of stamps divided by the gutter margin between them (see also *Inter Panneau*).

Hairline. A fine diagonal line across the corner background to the check letters of Great Britain stamps printed 1863–4. It only occurs on fourpence, sixpence and ninepence values and was deliberately incorporated into the design in order to identify a particular silver surfaced plate which was being used instead of the more usual copper plate. The term used to describe the effect of a scratched plate as it appears on the printed stamp.

Half Lengths. Popular name for the first issues of Victoria (the Australian State) which show a half-length portrait of Queen Victoria.

Half-Tone. A picture or illustration, reproduced in one colour only, giving variations in light and shade. By translating the varying tones in a picture or photograph into dots of varying sizes the picture can be litho printed. The process of transfer is known as screening.

Hand Made Paper. Paper made sheet by sheet in moulds by craftsmen. It is usually recognisable by the deckle edges, and the likely variations in thickness and texture on a single sheet,

Handstamp. A postmark, overprint, *cachet* or other such mark applied to a stamp or postal item by hand.

Handstruck. Similar to a handstamp but restricted in the main to: 1) Describing stamps produced singly from a handheld die. 2) The postal markings indicating postage has been paid, particularly in pre-adhesive days.

Harrow Perforations. A means of perforating a complete *pane* or sheet with one stroke of the peforator. It is so called because the setting of the pins resembles a harrow used in the fields. The stamps at the edge of the sheets peforated by this method very often have one side imperforate and corner stamps two sides imperforate.

Hatching. A method of creating a dark area on a stamp by the use of parallel and crossed lines of engraving on the plate. In recess printing the closer or deeper the lines are engraved the darker the effect.

Hawid Mount. A special type of mount used to mount mint stamps without damaging the gum. A gummed backing sheet has sealed to it along the bottom edge a thin sheet of clear plastic. The stamp rests behind the clear plastic and the whole mount is stuck to the album page.

Head. 1) The part of a perforating machine which makes the perforation holes. 2) A reference to the head portrayed on a stamp, very often in comparison with another of the same person but drawn differently or in a different pose.

Head Plate. Where more than one plate is required to print the stamp, the head plate is that which prints the portrait. The part of the design including the value is printed by the *duty plate*.

Health Stamp. A charity postage stamp issued annually by New Zealand on which the proceeds from the surcharge go to the George V Memorial Children's Health Camp Federation.

Heavy Cancel. A cancellation on a stamp which reduces any value the stamp may have (except to a postmark collector) because it defaces the stamp much more than is usual on that particular issue.

Helecon. A substance added to the paper of some Australian stamps used in conjunction with automatic letter facing machines (see *Fluorescence*).

Helicopter Mail. Mail which has been officially carried by helicopter and which bears a *cachet* or other evidence of this fact.

Hermes. The Greek god of commerce who was both messenger and herald to the Gods, and who has been featured on stamps of several countries, notably Greece. Very often confused with Mercury who was the Roman equivalent.

Hidden Dates. On some Canadian stamps the date of printing is incorporated as a minute part of the design very often only visible under a glass if one knows where to look. It was presumably a security device and an aid in detecting forgeries (see *secret mark*).

Hill. Sir Rowland Hill was the great British postal reformer of the nineteenth century whose efforts led to the introduction of the Uniform Penny Post and the widepread use of adhesive stamps to prepay the postage.

Hinge. A small rectangle of paper gummed on one side used for fixing stamps on album pages. A good quality hinge may be removed without damaging the stamp, thus allowing re-arrangement of a collection from time to time. Poor quality hinges which do not permit this should be avoided.

Mint stamps which have been mounted in this way are known as "mounted mint" as compared with "unmounted mint" or "mint, never hinged" etc. Such a description may be further qualified by the use of terms such as "hinge remainders", "heavy hinge" etc. describing to some extent the condition at the back.

Hingeless. Refers to an album the pages of which have mounts already provided in which stamps may be placed without the need to use a hinge.

Hold To Light (HTL). A description of picture postcards which need to be held up in front of a light in order to see the picture. These may be either cut-outs, where the picture is formed by the parts which are left, or metamorphic, where by moving the card in relation to the light the picture or colour appears to change.

Holes. Some stamps have legitimately had holes punched in them to perform an authorised use. For example, stamps of Western Australia so punched were used by government departments. Generally any unauthorised hole in a stamp, even a minute pinhole, will reduce its value (see *Perfins*).

Hotel Posts. 1) An official post office set up in a hotel providing the usual facilities. Mail may be identified only by the cancellation. 2) An unofficial service for the conveyance of mail to the nearest post office set up by hoteliers, initially in Switzerland, who issued their own stamps for the service. Such mail also required the regular postage stamps for carriage through the normal postal channels and is therefore easily recognisable.

Imitation Perforations. Pseudo perforations printed in the gutters between stamps.

Imperf or Imperforate. A stamp without perforations or *roulette* and which would therefore have to be cut from the sheet using scissors. Commonly called imperfs, they should be collected with margins as large as possible.

The side of a stamp which is imperforate is also described as imperf. It is normal on many coil stamps for the sides to be imperf since the stamps will only be torn in one direction across the strip along the perforations provided.

Imperforate errors fall into several categories and should

always be collected in a proving multiple if necessary. Examples include stamps which are normally perforated but which have missed being perforated altogether. These will therefore be imperf on all four sides. A *singleton* should have margins wide enough all round to show that there is no possibility of the perforations having been trimmed off.

"Imperf between" indicates a pair of stamps with the gutter between them imperforate. A stamp with only one side imperf may have come either from a booklet where very often the outside edges are deliberately imperf or from the edge of a sheet where it was common not to perforate the outside edge of the stamps. Such marginal stamps are sometimes called fantails. Beware also *wing margin* copies which have been trimmed (see *Straight Edge*).

Imperium Essays. De La Rue prepared a series of essays using the *key plate* designs of Queen Victoria but with the word "Imperium" in place of the name of the country. They were printed in various colour combinations to show the effect and availability to colonies ordering stamps.

Impression. The image of the design from the *master die* transferred by pressure to the surface of the transfer roller or the printing plate.

Imprimatur. On early British issues one imperforate sheet of stamps from the first printing was registered and preserved in Somerset House as part of the postal archives. Stamps were cut from these sheets for various reasons and these are known as imprimaturs.

Imprint. 1) The printer's name, address or other identifying mark printed in the sheet margin. A block of stamps attached to the margin which contains the full imprint is known as an Imprint Block (see *Cylinder block*). 2) The engraver's or designer's name, initials or other mark which may be incorporated into, or appear below the design of the stamp.

India Letter. A letter carried on an East India Company vessel which was appropriately handstamped to indicate that fact at the port of entry into the British Isles.

India Paper. A very thin soft paper used for taking proofs. It is generally made from bamboo fibres and emanates from China or Japan.

Inflation Issues. Stamps issued during periods of hyper-inflation. The face values of such issues reach enormous amounts as the value of the currency decreases. Some inflation stamps merely carry an overprint to indicate their postal use, and where bought at the rate that applied on any particular day for that service.

Ink. The liquid which is transferred from the reservoir on the printing press, via the printing plate to the paper where it forms the design of the stamp. Ink, like most colouring agents, fades if left in direct sunlight, may change colour due to atmospheric or chemical conditions, or runs into the fibres of the paper if it gets wet. Any of these things happening will spoil the stamp and reduce its philatelic value.

Inscription. 1) The words or characters which form a part of the stamp design. 2) Marginal inscriptions are all the words or characters which appear in the sheet margins (see *Imprint*).

Inserted By Hand. Correction or other mark made directly onto the printing plate to rectify some omission on the *master die*.

Intaglio. Line engraved or recess printing. Intaglio is the Italian for carving or indentation, hence "cutting out". Thus the design required is cut out of the die, and the printed area of the stamp comes from the ink held in the recessed areas of the plate.

Intermediate Perforation. A perforation which is not one hundred percent clean but which is much better than *rough*.

International Reply Coupon. A coupon bought at a post office in one country which may be exchanged at the post office in another for a postage stamp covering the foreign rate for a single weight letter. A Commonwealth reply coupon performs a similar function but is only usable at post offices of countries in the British Commonwealth.

Inter-Provisionals. The name given to stamps of the individual provinces of South Africa which became valid for postage anywhere within the Union after May 31st 1910. South Africa did not issue a full range of stamps until 1913 and therefore inter-provisionals used other than in the home state and postmarked with a clear date for the intervening period are very collectable.

Inter-Panneau. The gutter margin between two panes of a sheet was very often inscribed with a decorative pattern. Pairs or blocks of stamps containing such gutters are known as inter-panneau.

Interrupted Perforation. Perforation where the spaces between the holes are uneven, very often made so deliberately to reduce a tendency for the paper to split.

Interspace. In some printing and perforating formats a *blind stamp* is left between two others or between a stamp and the sheet margin.

Invalidated. 1) A stamp which has been cancelled in some way to prevent its re-use. 2) A stamp which has been *demonetised*.

Inverted. Describes a feature of a stamp which has been printed upside-down in error. Hence either the frame or the centre of a stamp printed from two plates, or where the plate is created from two dies, may be inverted. Inverted overprints occur because the sheets of stamps have been fed into the press the wrong way round. Inverted watermarks may or may not be errors depending upon the make-up of the sheet. They can be caused by the paper being set the wrong way round or becoming folded in the press. Many came from special plates used for printing booklet stamps. Collectors aways try to show a stamp with an inverted feature alongside a correctly printed one for comparison.

Irregular Perforation. Perforation where the size of the holes, or the spacing between the holes varies or is out of alignment.

Italic. Description of a particular type-face with sloping letters.

Item. A single stamp, cover or other object which has philatelic interest and is described in a catalogue or advertisement. Items in the plural may indicate a mixture including covers and cards, pieces, individual stamps etc.

Ivory Head. The light or uncoloured outline of the head of Queen Victoria against the normal bluish colouring of the paper when seen from the back. This occurred on early line engraved issues of Great Britain. It was caused because the ink in the much lighter parts of the engraving for the Queen's head did not produce such a marked blueing effect as did the ink in the areas of heavy engraving which form the frame and background. Also a stamp having such a feature.

Japanese Paper. Made from the bark of the mulberry tree in Japan. Sometimes known as native paper. It was used for the *Cherry Blossom* issues of Japan.

Join. A paper join. Usually found on coil pairs or strips which have been made up from sheets as opposed to being printed as a continuous roll.

Jubilee Line. The name given to the line which is printed in the margin around the sheet, so called because its first use occurred in Queen Victoria's jubilee year. The intention was to provide a protection to prevent damage to the edge of the plate. Jubilee lines are described as continuous when there is no break in the line, or co-extensive when a break occurs corresponding with the gutters between the stamps. Various marks in the jubilee lines enable collectors to identify particular plates or printings.

Jubilee Issue. 1) Stamp issued to commemorate a jubilee. 2) Name given erroneously to the Great Britain *definitives* of 1887, which was Queen Victoria's jubilee year.

Key Plate. In stamps having the same design on all values and printed from two plates, the key plate prints the general or common part of the design leaving space for the *duty plate* to print in the value. Also known as the *head plate*.

Key Type. Many colonial territories used a standard stamp design with only the name and value being different. Such designs are known as key types and are usually given particular names by which they are referred to in catalogues and by collectors.

Killer. A name descriptive of the cancellors (and their effects) used to cancel stamps before the introduction of modern machine cancelling equipment. The object was to prevent a stamp's re-use, which they achieve very effectively, much to the chagrin of collectors searching for a fine used specimen.

Kiloware. Stamps of one country on paper sold by weight and generally containing common current stamps as used on commercial correspondence. Better and luxury grades are available but cost more. A useful source for the variety hunter or postmark collector (see *Bank lot*).

Label. 1) The original name for a postage stamp, very often used in marginal inscriptions. 2) Any adhesive which does not have postal validity including a postage due, *bogus* issue, *etiquette*, souvenir item etc. 3) That part of a booklet pane on which an advertisement or other message is printed.

Labelled Stamp. A stamp to which a label is attached carrying a message, advertisement or instruction (see *tabs*).

Lady McLeod. A popular name for the first issue of Trinidad, in 1847, which showed an impression of the *SS Lady McLeod* over the initials "LMcL". They were issued by the owner, David Bryce, for prepayment for the carriage of letters on the vessel between San Fernando and Port of Spain.

Laid Paper. Paper showing a watermark of closely spaced parallel lines in one direction, produced by the closeness of the wires making up the *dandy roll*. Stamps are described as printed on vertical or horizontal laid paper depending upon the direction of the lines in relation to the printed design of the stamp.

Late Fee Stamp. A stamp affixed to a letter to indicate that an additional fee has been paid in order to allow that item to catch (or catch up) a particular mail even though normal closing time for the mail has passed.

Laureated Issue. A popular name for the 1851–54 stamp of New South Wales on which the Queen is portrayed wearing a laurel wreath. Also applied to French stamps of 1862–70 showing Napolean III similarly wreathed.

Letter Card. A folded card, allowing the letter to be written on one side, which when closed is sealed with adhesive round the edges. The edges are usually perforated for easy opening by the addressee. It usually bears an imprinted stamp and may be bought at post offices, the price includes both the postage and the cost of the stationery.

Letter Post. The postal service provided for the carriage of letters as compared with parcels, printed matter or other items.

Letterpress. A method of printing where the inked surface from which the print is taken is raised up from the rest of the plate. The opposite of recess printing (see *surface printing* and *typography*).

Lift. 1) To remove an adhesive from a cover or the paper to which it adheres. 2) A technical term in colour printing to indicate a quality of the printing. Lack of lift indicates a flat effect lacking highlights.

Line Block. 1) A printing plate which can only produce lines or areas of solid colour (see *half-tone*). 2) A marginal block of stamps showing the *jubilee line* or other marginal lines (see *arrow block*).

Line Engraving. An engraving process whereby lines or slivers of metal are removed from the *master die* corresponding to the design to be printed. Since the ink which will print the design will fill these lines or engraved areas, it follows that the deeper the engraving or the closer together the lines, the darker will be the effect on the printed design. *Intaglio* and *recess printing* are other names for printing using this principle.

Line Pair. American coil stamps have a line printed at regular intervals between two stamps, very often the twentieth or twenty-fifth stamp. Pairs of stamps showing the line are known as line pairs and may command a premium on the normal price.

Line Perforation. Perforation is completed one line at a time in one direction, after which the sheets are turned through ninety degrees and are then perforated, again one line at a time, at right angles to the first perforation. This results in irregular corners on the stamps since the corner holes will rarely coincide exactly. Rotary perforators may perforate all the lines in one direction with one operation of the machine (see *Comb perforation*).

Lithography or Litho. A printing process whereby ink corresponding to the colourless portions of the design is rejected from the plate by the use of the repellent action of water, leaving ink adhering on the plate only where the design requires it. This impression is then transferred to the paper either directly or via a blanket roller. (This process is commonly known as offset printing.) The use of a rubber blanket roller means that a rougher surfaced paper may be used than printing directly from a metal plate would allow, whilst still maintaining the quality of the printing. Stamps printed by lithography feel flat when compared to stamps recess printed where the ink sits on the surface of the paper.

Local Prints. Stamps printed in a colony to distinguish them from other issues of the same design which may have been printed in the parent country previously.

Local Stamp. A postage stamp whose use is restricted to a specified area, such as a town or route where an official postal service does not operate, and which is not valid in the official postal service outside the area specified. Such items as posts operating within the Oxford and Cambridge Universities, the Russian rural posts (called *Zemstvos*) or services operated by an island landlord to the mainland are classed as locals and many collectors form extensive collections of such issues.

London Prints. Refers to printings of colonial stamps printed in London as distinct from printings of the same stamps which were made in the colony itself. Among the better known are some early issues of New Zealand, South Africa and Western Australia. Various differences of paper, shades, perforation or watermark may assist collectors in determining to which printing a stamp may belong.

Loose Letter. A letter arriving at an office of delivery without any indication of the office of origin.

Lozenge Cancellation. Cancellation in the shape of a diamond usually of bars or dots, found on many early French stamps.

Lozenge Perforation. Perforation which removes a diamond-shaped piece of paper from the hole instead of the usual round one.

Luminescence. The American equivalent of *phosphor*, another means of "tagging" stamps for use with high speed sorting machines. In this instance different luminescent afterglow colours enable the machines to distinguish between airmail and regular (surface) mail (see *fluorescence*).

Machin. The popular name for the second series of Queen Elizabeth II *definitives* of Great Britain, named after Arnold Machin, whose bust of the Queen was used as a model for the head. There are two main series. Pre-decimal Machins are those with face values in pounds, shillings and pence (£sd), and decimal Machins those with face values are in decimal currency.

There are also high values and regional issues as well. There have been a considerable number of different printings in the series involving changes of colour, paper, positioning of the phosphor bands, phosphorised papers and even three kinds of gum. Specialists recognise different heads and also positions of the value in relation to the head. The *Connoisseur* catalogue is generally considered to be the best specialised catalogue covering all aspects of these issues.

Machine Cancel. A postmark made by a machine to cancel the stamp on a letter or card. It usually consists of two parts of which one is a date stamp and the other may be wavy lines, slogan, flag or bars etc. (see *Duplex*).

Mackennal. A popular name for the second George V *definitives* of Great Britain which showed the king's head in profile. They (the heads) were designed by Bertram Mackennal but should not be confused with the *Downeys* which were also designed by him.

Magic Card. A picture postcard which only reveals the picture when heat or friction is applied.

Magnifier. An absolute must for the serious collector. They range from a simple hand-held magnifying glass, or a more elaborate type with built-in illumination, to full size microscopes. Some such as a watchmaker's glass or a magnifier which is tripod-mounted allow the collector to use both hands.

Mailometer Perforations. Perforations to USA stamps between 1906–17 made privately by the Mail-O-Meter Co. on stamps for use in vending machines.

Make-up. 1) The format, contents and sequence of panes in a booklet. 2)   The position of the impressions or panes on a plate.

Maltese Cross. 1) A distinctive eight-pointed cross used by the Knights of Malta formed by joining four isosceles triangles by their points in the centre. Also known as "Cross Pattée" or "Croix Paté". Very often used in the designs of stamps and also as a watermark. 2) A popular name for the first cancellations used on Great Britain adhesives in 1840, although most of them tend to resemble a rosette rather more than the true cross. Many different examples have been recognised by collectors including those in use at the London chief office which had numerals running from 1 to 12 in the centre. Maltese cross cancellations are found mainly in red and black on the 1840 issues and in black on the 1841 issues. Other colours are also found but command premium prices.

Manilla Paper. Paper originally made from Manilla hemp, usually pale brown and used extensively for envelopes, especially larger sizes, and wrappers.

Manuscript. Any mark written by hand on a stamp or cover.

Manuscript Cancellation. Cancellation of a stamp by hand using a pen, pencil or other indelible writing instrument. Generally known as *pen cancels,* many indicate fiscal rather than postal use.

Margin. 1) The unprinted area around the edge of a stamp (see *gutter* which is the unprinted space between two stamps). Large even margins on an imperforate stamp are sought after by collectors and will enhance its value. 2) The area around the edge of a pane or sheet of stamps. Many contain printing such as the printer's name, plate or cylinder numbers, value of the sheet, sheet number, *jubilee lines*, etc.

Marginal Inscription. Any printing appearing in the margin of a sheet of stamps.

Marginal Rule. The line or lines printed in the margins parallel to the edges of the stamps very often known as *jubilee lines*.

Maritime Mail. Mail posted on board ships at sea and which usually carries a distinctive cancellation or *cachet* to that effect. The words "Paquebot", "Posted at Sea" and variations always indicate such usage, as may the name of the ship.

Matched Pair. Describes two stamps from the same position on the same plate but which come from different and distinctive printings, usually in different colours. Most often refers to the Great Britain Penny Blacks and Penny Reds of 1840 and 1841 where the first Penny Reds were printed using the original Penny Black plates.

Matched Set. Describes a set of the four corner blocks of the same stamp showing the same plate number in each corner, a very popular way of collecting in North America. The blocks are usually mounted in the layout of a miniature sheet.

Maximum Card. A picture postcard on which the picture matches that of the adhesive attached to it, very often cancelled with a related or first day postmark.

Medallion. A popular name for the second issue of Belgium in 1849 which showed the portrait of King Leopold I in an oval frame (see *Epaulettes*).

Mercury. The Roman god who was the herald and messenger of the gods (equivalent to the Greek *Hermes*). His head appears on French and Austrian stamps of which the most famous is the rare "Red Mercury", a newspaper stamp issued by Austria in 1856.

Merson. A renowned French artist who designed the higher-value stamps first issued in 1900 and which are known as "Mersons".

Mesh. A term used to describe certain watermarks which show a mesh of lines rather like wire netting.

Metal Currency Stamps. Stamps which may only be purchased against payment in gold or silver.

Metallic. 1) Ink in a metallic colour which dries with a shiny or metallic surface. 2) A stamp on which a metallic foil has been used as part of the design.

Metered Mail. Mail which has been franked, to indicate postage has been paid, by a machine which records the amount of postage or the number of items franked. Commercial franking machines have a meter into which has been set the amount of postage which has been prepaid. This meter always shows how much postage remains unused, and very often how much has been used cumulatively through that meter to that date. The franks may be applied either directly to the envelope or to an adhesive tape ready for affixing to more bulky items. The frank itself includes a date stamp, a meter identification number, the value franked, and very often an advertisement for the company using it. Post Office franked mail normally shows the word "Paid" or "Official Paid" sometimes as part of a date stamp.

Michel. A well known German publisher of catalogues for German and European stamps.

Mileage Mark. A postal mark which includes a number

indicative of the distance of the place named either from the capital or some central reference point. In Britain such marks indicated "miles". On the Continent however, they very often showed *Rayons* which were radial bands from a central point and adhesives for the appropriate rates showed "Rayons" and the number.

Millésime. Marginal marking in use between 1876 and 1926 on sheets of French stamps to indicate the year of printing. A Millésime pair indicates a *gutter pair* with the millésime printed on the gutter margin between the two stamps. Their use was similar to the control numbers on Great Britain issues.

Miniature Sheet. A sheet of stamps specially printed to include one of each commemorative set or a small number (sometimes only one) of a single denomination, and which has its own sheet margins very often containing an imprint or other information, even advertisements. Originally issued in connection with or only at exhibitions, they are now widely issued by many countries and whilst postally valid are really aimed at the philatelic market. As with all other stamps, miniature sheets are found perforated, imperforate, watermarked or unwatermarked, missing colours, with special overprints and all other varieties and errors. Many miniature sheets, because of their size and lack of perforations, are not really practical for postal use and such sheets are regarded more as *souvenir sheets* although they should not be confused with them.

Mint. Indicates a gummed stamp which retains its gum and has no cancellations, i.e. it has not been used for its original intended purpose of prepaying the postage of a postal item onto which it has been stuck.

There are various degrees of mint recognised by philatelists and which affect the value of any particular stamp. 1) "Unmounted mint", "unhinged mint", "mint, never hinged". A stamp whose gum has no trace of any disturbances, hinge mark or hinge remainder and no paper adhering to the back. Such terms are sometimes qualified to describe gum cracking or crazed or a crease or bend. 2) "Mounted mint"; the stamp has been mounted and shows the mark(s) or the remains of the hinge(s) on the back. "Lightly mounted mint" is used where the hinge is negligible or where the single original hinge is still lightly attached to the stamp (see *condition, gum, hinge, unused*).

Misplaced. A term used to signify that the feature, letter, overprint, or colour is out of alignment with the remainder of the design. On early stamps of Great Britain misplaced letters are vital clues to identifying the particular plate number of the stamp in question. In modern printing a misplaced colour can produce startling effects on the design of the stamps although such colour shifts rarely gain catalogue status.

Mixed Franking. Cover bearing: 1) Stamps of more than one country, 2) Stamps of one country from more than one reign, 3) Stamps and *meter franks*; which combine to make up the postage for the route followed by the cover.

Mixed Perforation. A stamp which has been patched after incorrect perforation (usually badly misplaced) and reperforated correctly, sometimes with a different gauge.

Mixture. A dealer's description for loose unsorted stamps, (sometimes still on small pieces of the original envelope) from many countries, sometimes part sorted into categories such as large pictorials, British Commonwealth, Scandinavian etc. (see *Kiloware, Bank Lot*).

Mobile Post Offices. Postal facilities provided in mobile units such as caravans or specially converted vehicles and used temporarily outdoors at exhibitions, showgrounds etc. Mail posted will generally receive a distinctive cancellation or *cachet*. In some countries mobile posting facilities are provided on trains or buses and may be identifiable only by the cancellations.

Moiré. A security device in the form of close wavy lines sometimes printed on the backs of stamps.

Montage. Usually a picture postcard bearing stamps which have been cut up and then stuck down to form the design or picture.

Mormon Stamps. A bogus issue supposed to be been issued by the Mormons in Salt Lake City in 1852. This was denied by Brigham Young, their leader, whose portrait appeared on the stamps.

Mouchon. Popular name for French stamps of 1900 and redrawn designs of 1904 after their designer and engraver Eugène Mouchon.

Mount. The means by which stamps and philatelic items are retained in position on the album page. Before the development of the modern hingeless methods the mount was usually a stamp *hinge* although strictly speaking a mount was a small square of cardboard (very often black) on which the stamp was mounted. This mount was then hinged into the album and when the stamp was moved the whole mount was moved, thus avoiding the necessity of removing the hinge from the back of the stamp. This was both bulky in the album and time consuming, and with the introduction of modern stamp hinges was regarded as unnecessary.

Recent developments, particularly for mint stamps, have been the Hawid strips, the Hagner system, Showcard and Prinz mounts (among others) which use a plastic pocket system either bonded to the album page or with adhesive at the back so that they may be mounted to suit the collector.

Mourning. 1) Stamps with the black borders, either printed specially or overprinted on existing stamps, issued in mourning for heads of state or other national leaders. 2) Envelopes printed with black edges which form a popular collecting group. Generally speaking, the wider the black band the more closely related the user is to the deceased.

Mulready. The name given to Great Britain prepaid postal stationery issued in 1840 and designed by William Mulready. The patriotic designs suffered considerable criticism and were parodied and lampooned so much that their use was discontinued after a very short time.

Multi-Lingual. Stamps on which more than one language is inscribed or overprinted to meet the needs of mixed populations speaking different languages within one country, or of an occupying government (see *bilingual*)

Multiple. A term descriptive of both stamps, watermarks and perforations etc. 1) A single stamp made up of several smaller units. 2) Two or more stamps joined together in a strip, block or other shape. 3) A watermark in which the device is repeated throughout the sheet in close proximity, very often staggered or alternating so that it falls on the stamps haphazardly. (As opposed to a single or simple watermark in which the device is designed to show once only in the middle of every stamp.)

4) Perforator which perforates several lines at a single stroke.
5) In printing, the use of a transfer consisting of several stamp designs which is used to build up a sheet more quickly than using a single transfer.

Multipositive. A photographic glass plate used in the production of the printing plate in photogravure printing.

Mutilation. Some countries' postal authorities, notably Afghanistan, rendered stamps unfit for further postal use by tearing a corner off after they had been applied to the envelope.

National Philatelic Society (NPS). Originally founded as the Junior Philatelic Society in 1899.

Native Paper. A locally made paper mainly used in some Indian states and Oriental countries. The texture, quality and thickness vary considerably.

Network. A security pattern of crossed or wavy lines printed on stamp paper (see *Burélage*).

Never Hinged (N/H). In popular usage in North America for *unmounted mint*.

New Issue Service. Many dealers provide this service in varying degrees, enabling collectors to obtain new issues of any country as they are issued. Individual postal authorities also provide similar services for stamps of that country (and related territories). The best services provide for not only stamps but postal stationery, miniature sheets, printing variations and provisional issues. A fee varying between 20% to 30% is usually charged on the face value of the items bought (or on the cost if the item is particularly elusive).

Newspaper Stamps. Many countries allow newspapers to travel though the post at special reduced rates. Newspaper stamps are issued to prepay the postage.

New Year Stamps. Special stamps issued to celebrate a New Year, either Western or Oriental calendars (cf. Christmas and Easter stamps).

Nibbed Perf. Description of a perforation tooth which has been pulled and thus looks like the end of a pen nib with a slight split or indentation at the tip (see *Short perf.*).

Normal (N). Used as an abbreviation to indicate normal (prices) so that a variety may be valued at 2N (twice normal), 5N (five times) etc.

Not for Use. Overprint on one stamp of a pane of six in a Natal booklet. The penny lost in the value of the stamps purchased represented the amount charged for the booklet.

Numbered Stamps. 1) Some Spanish stamps from 1875 onwards have the sheet number printed on the back, i.e. the number is the same on all the stamps from the same sheet but changes from sheet to sheet. Stamps with all zeros which come from the specimen sheet are much sought after. 2) Some stamps of Uruguay and Estonia had a number incorporated into the design and were numbered in rotation on the sheet. 3) Many Great Britain stamps of Queen Victoria's reign had the plate number included in the design but these are more often referred to as "penny (or two penny) plates", or "surface printed issues".

Obligatory Tax Stamp. Fund raising stamp required to be used on letters in addition to normal postage stamps. The compulsory use may be restricted to certain times or periods or may reflect the delivery requirement, e.g. Sunday delivery. The funds raised are usually associated with a well known (in the country) charity or international organisation.

Obliteror, Obliteration. 1) An overprint on a stamp designed to obliterate or block out certain parts of the original design, e.g. the portrait of a deposed monarch or leader. 2) The device used to cancel a stamp to prevent its re-use. Many early obliterators were *dumb* and consisted of bars or blocks which literally obliterated the design of the stamp, much to the disgust of collectors today looking for clear but light cancellations. Many obliterations are known by the names based on their appearance such as Maltese cross, barred oval, target, grid-irons etc., and when heavily used are termed *killers*.

Obsolete. Stamps withdrawn from sale at post offices, though they may still be valid for postage (see *Demonetised* or *Invalidated*).

Occupational stamps. Specially printed or, more commonly, overprinted stamps for use in occupied territories by forces or political movements.

Octagonal. A stamp or cancel having eight sides. In the case of stamps they may be imperforate, perforated square or perforated to shape. Imperforate stamps are conisdered more valuable *cut square* than cut to shape.

Off-Centre. A stamp having poor centring.

Official. Special stamps, or ordinary stamps overprinted, for use by government departments. The word official may appear in some form although some countries used letter abbreviations to denote official usage or the appropriate department using the stamps. Official stamps are not authorised for use on private letters nor should mint examples be available to the general public.

Some countries have used *perfins* to indicate official usage and although these tend to be listed only in specialised catalogues, many collectors quite rightly regard them as legitimate items for inclusion of their collections.

Official Paid. Special cancellation indicating a government, post office or other authorised departmental letter on which the postage has been pre-paid.

Off-set. 1) A term used to describe a particular type of lithography, in which the impression is first off-set from the plate onto a roller which then transfers it to the paper. 2) The transference during printing or part of the design or surplus ink to the gummed side of another stamp (usually a mirror image). It may enhance the value of the stamp. 3) The picking up on the gum of a mint stamp of some printing impression from another stamp or illustration on an album page etc., usually due to poor storage conditions. This usually reduces the value of the stamp. 4) A term indicating that a feature of a design or overprint is out of line with the main design.

Olympics. Refers to all stamps, first day covers and other items relating to the Olympic Games. A very popular field of collecting with even the smallest stamp issuing countries issuing stamps to commemorate either the games or some success in them. In recent years the increasing cost of staging the games has lead to many *charity stamps* being issued to augment hard pressed budgets, both for national team support and for the provision of stadia and other facilities by the host nation.

Omnibus Issue. Commemoratives or special stamps issued simultaneously for a particular event, by a number of countries, very often using the same or similar designs. Examples include coronation, jubilee, Europa, Unesco and ILO, Red Cross and human rights and many others.

On/Off Paper. Generally used when describing bulk material.
On paper: the stamps are still attached to part of the original envelope or wrapping paper.
Off paper: The stamps have been removed (lifted, floated, soaked etc.) from the original envelope or wrapping paper.
On piece: a single item retained on piece (and tied to it) by reason of an interesting postmark or other cancellation, or combination of stamps etc., and which will remain in that state when mounted in a collection or for display.

Ordinary (O). A term used to distinguish "ordinary" paper or printing from *chalk surfaced paper* or *phosphor* printings.

Original Gum (OG). Most often found as the abbreviation. A mint stamp having most (part OG) or all (full OG) remaining although this may be marked or hidden by hinge remainders, paper adherence etc. This term probably causes more headaches for both the dealer, auctioneer and collector and generally speaking should be used in conjunction with further description such as "heavy hinge", "hinge remainders" etc. to avoid mis-understanding.

Overland Mail. Mail forwarded to and from India, Australia and the Far East via Egypt before the Suez Canal was opened. This was quicker than the long sea route round the Cape of Good Hope. There was a similar service linking the Persian Gulf with the Eastern Mediterranean.

Overprint. Anything subsequently printed on the face of a stamp to change or restrict its usage or to commemorate a particular event, but which does not alter its value (see *Surcharge*). Many examples exist but some of the most common are: 1) To allow a fiscal to be used for postage. 2) To allow a postage stamp to be used fiscally. 3) To restrict the use of the stamp to government departments (see *Officials*). 4) For mourning stamps. 5) First issues following the change of name of the issuing country before properly named stamps can be produced. 6) Commemoration of events which may not have allowed sufficient time for specially designed commemoratives to be produced. 7) For security reasons after stamp thefts or forgeries have been discovered. 8) To allow stamps of one country to be used in another (see *Occupation stamps*).

Oxidised. The effect of air, dampness and sunlight on the ink of a stamp. In the cases of a red or orange stamp, the colour tends to go deep or darkish brown. This can be reversed to some extent by applying a weak solution of hydrogen peroxide though this may harm the stamp in other ways and may not be permanent.

Packet. 1) Originally the word for a mail-carrying vessel operating to a regular timetable over a specific route, wind and weather permitting. Mail carried on such vessels was usually postmarked "Packet Letter". Rates were generally higher than *ship letters*. 2) A designation for the foreign mail service slightly cheaper than letter post but more expensive than parcel post, more correctly called "small packet post". It is particularly useful for items of small value, bulky documents etc. The service is available either at surface or airmail rates, and items sent may also be registered if required. 3) The transparent envelope used for protecting stamps when being transmitted from one person to another, or when in storage. 4) An assortment of stamps, sold by dealers. Dealers' packets may be made up by country, set, theme or quantity. 5) The name given in philatelic societies to the box of exchange or club booklets which is circulated to members.

Pair. Two stamps still joined together either horizontally or vertically. If the sheet gutter runs between them they are known as a *gutter pair*.

Pane. 1) Part of a sheet of stamps, usually a half or a quarter, in regular layout, divided from the other panes of the sheet by *gutter margins*. 2) A page of stamps in a booklet, including any labels which may form part of it.

Panel Card. A picture postcard printed on very thick card.

Pantograph. A draftsman's instrument (adapted by engravers and designers for use in printing) by means of which a flat design may be copied, usually in reduced scale.

Paper. The medium upon which the design of the stamp is

printed. Many different types of paper have been used for postage stamps, some of them experimental, others used during emergency because of shortages. However, most fall into one of two categories: laid (which shows a pattern of lighter parallel lines running through it) and wove (which shows no particular pattern). The characteristics of a paper determine its suitability for stamp production since it must at the same time provide a fine surface to receive the printed impression by the printing method adopted; be able to hold the ink permanently both of the stamp and the cancellation in order to prevent removal or forgery; to be strong enough to stand up to public usage but be easily and conveniently separated when perforated. Readers are referred to individual entries for particular types of paper throughout the book.

Paper Fault. Any irregularity or impurity in the paper as delivered from the mill.

Papermaker. There have been many papermakers whose paper has been used for stamp printing. In philately the term applies to a paper in which the papermaker's name appears as a watermark (known as papermaker's watermark) either through the sheet or in the margin and which may or may not be visible on the stamps.

Papier-Mâché. A hard strong substance made of pulp or layers of paper mixed with paste or size and sometimes used in the process of plate making (see *Stereotype*).

Paquebot. The term officially adopted by the Universal Postal Union in 1897 to describe mail posted on board a ship. Such mail is usually postmarked with a cancel including the word "Paquebot", very often augmented by the words "posted at sea". It will be accepted at all ports of call of the ship and may bear stamps from a country different from that of the port of landing.

Parachute Mail. Mail dropped by parachute from passing aircraft to islands or other isolated locations, and usually identifiable by a *cachet* or other inscription.

Paraph. A flourish or embellishment of initials or signature much used on signet rings and seals, and sometimes appearing in the design of stamps or overprints.

Parcel Stamp. A stamp especially produced to prepay postage on parcels. Although some postal authorities issued parcel stamps, in many countries local parcels are carried in the main by private companies who issue their own stamps. These locals are of interest to collectors but are usually missing from the general catalogues. Many railway companies have carried parcels and issued their own railway parcel stamps. Many other countries use the regular postage stamps for the collection of the fees on parcel post and usually have a distinctive cancellation in use for such mail. Parcel cancellations are usually heavy and unsightly and collectors place less value on a stamp having one than on a stamp with a clear circular date stamp.

Part Perforated. Stamps only partly perforated due to some fault in the perforating and which have been sold by the Post Office to the public. Such stamps might have one or more sides partly or completely imperforate. The term would not be applied to booklet or coil stamps issued normally with one or more sides imperforate or having straight edges since these are intended to be in this form.

Patriotic. 1) An envelope illustrated with a patriotic theme very often issued in wartime to help raise morale. 2) Picture postcards usually showing, in addition to some national event, the flag or other emblem of the country concerned. 3) Some postmarks, such as the flag postmark of Canada, may also be regarded as patriotic whether used on a patriotic cover or postcard or on an otherwise plain envelope.

PD. A handstamp applied to covers indicating "postage paid to destination". Do not confuse with same abbreviation PD sometimes used for *postage due stamps*.

Peace And Commerce. A popular name for the French stamp design issued first in France in 1876 and the French Colonies in 1877 and which continued in use with new issue until 1900.

Peacocks. A popular name for George VI stamps of Burma overprinted by the Japanese with the peacock design, the Japanese Royal emblem.

Pelure Paper. A very thin, often brittle paper, usually fairly transparent and used on some early issues.

Pen Cancelled. Strictly speaking, stamps postally used which have been cancelled by the postal authorities using pen and ink (or modern ball pen) or indelible pencil. In some countries this was the normal practice, in others it was used either at very small offices without hand cancellors, or to cancel stamps which had missed the cancellor.

A large number of pen-marked stamps have however been used for fiscal purposes, the pen-mark usually being part of a signature and/or date, or other words used on a receipt, etc. The term pen-marked should properly be applied to such items.

Pence Issues. A popular name for the early £sd stamps of Canada and Ceylon used prior to the introduction of decimal currency.

Penny Black. The first adhesive postage stamp, issued in Great Britain on 1st May 1840. It was valid from 6th May 1840 to coincide with the introduction of the Uniform Penny Post. Because of difficulties with cancellations in colour, it was superceded within a year by the Penny Red in the same design which allowed black cancellations to be applied.

Penny Post. Postal service which carried letters within a certain area for one penny. The London Penny Post was set up by William Dockwra in 1680, but applied only to letters within London. Other cities also set up Penny Posts within their boundaries. Entires carried in these Penny Posts usually bear identifying postmarks and handstamps. The Uniform Penny Post set up by Rowland Hill in 1840 provided a service throughout the United Kingdom for letters under half an ounce to be carried at one penny each.

Percé. The French equivalent of *roulette* meaning quite literally pierced. Several types are recognised by collectors including: 1) Percé en arc – cuts of short curved arcs. The edge of the stamps appear scalloped. 2) Percé en ligne droit – The normal roulette made of short straight cuts. 3) Percé en losanges – The cuts are in the form of a cross. 4) Percé en points – The cuts are made by a series of pin pricks (but unlike pin perforation the paper is not removed). 5) Percé en scie – The cuts are made in a zig-zag line which gives the edges of the stamp the resemblance of saw teeth. 6) Percé en serpentine – Producing very pronounced teeth on the edges of the stamp like the multi-humped back of a serpent.

Perforated Initials (Perfins). Stamps with initials perforated in them. Mostly used by private companies or government departments for security reasons. Government use has been mainly of "OHMS" or "OS" but some postal authorities have also used the technique for producing specimen stamps. Generally speaking, normal stamps with commercial or unofficial perfins are of less value than the same stamps without, since collectors tend to regard them as less than perfect. In fact some perfined stamps are extremely rare and much sought after by specialists. There is a specialist society for perfin collectors.

Perforation. A means of making the separation of individual stamps easier by removing small pieces of paper from the gutters between the stamps. The size and number of holes may vary on each side of the stamp and will be determined by the direction of the grain and the strength of the paper, fewer or smaller holes being needed on the weaker edge.

Different methods of perforating a sheet may be adopted and are recognisable by collectors. They may be applied either with a flat bed operation or a rotary action. 1) Line perforation – where one or two parallel lines in one direction only are perforated with each pass of the machine. To perforate complete sheets the paper has to be turned through ninety degrees and perforated line by line in that direction also. 2) Comb perforation – where at least three sides of the stamp are perforated with each pass of the machine. The comb moves one stamp width before the next pass of the machine. The second pass completes the first stamp and perforates three sides of the second stamp. 3) Chambon perforation – a type of comb peforation which perforates one complete stamp and half of two sides of the two adjacent stamps. The comb then moves two stamps widths and the next pass completes the half perforated stamp. Where the registration is not exact a thicker or thinner tooth will be left at the centre of each side. 4) Harrow perforation – where a complete sheet is perforated with one pass of the machine. Sometimes the outer edge of the sheet is imperforate. 5) All-over perforation – for use on non-rectangular stamps such as triangular or circular stamps.

Perforations are further described firstly by reference to the size of the hole – large or small – and to the effectiveness of the blades or pins in removing the paper – clean or rough.

Perforations are measured by counting the number of holes in two centimetres. A perforation gauge makes this measurement an easy task, one of the best and most convenient being the Stanley Gibbons Instanta which consists of converging straight lines running long a scale printed on clear plastic.

Perkins, Bacon. The security printer, then called Perkins, Bacon and Petch, who printed the first adhesive stamp – the Penny Black. They have subsequently printed many millions of stamps for many different countries including such well known issues as the Chalons, the Cape Triangulars and the *Britannias*.

Personal Delivery Stamp. A stamp issued either to pre-pay the fee, or to indicate a fee was to be collected, for the item to be personally delivered only to the addressee.

Philatelic Agencies. Commercial companies who deal with publicity and sales of a postal authority's stamps in a given country or market area. In many cases this has included providing design and production control services. The oldest and most respected philatelic agent is the *Crown Agents* in London. Same countries recognising the value of the philatelic markets have overstepped the mark in the stámps produced and the marketing methods adopted, very often destroying the market they sought to develop. Collectors (and catalogue editors) are very much more aware of these particular instances and are quick to move away from collecting countries where they feel they are being unduly exploited.

Philatelic Traders Society (PTS). the leading British organisation for stamp dealers which not only issues guidelines on trading standards, provides advisory and legal services, but also considers the status of questionable issues and acts as a forum for collectors' complaints etc. Its symbol of membership indicates that the dealer concerned should act in accordance with its ethical and trading standards and to that extent provides a measure of protection to collectors.

Philately. Coined by M G Herpin, the term refers to stamp collecting in the widest sense. Rather obscurely from the Greek: Philo = friend, a = no, telos = tax, or a lover of something indicating no tax was due to be collected.

Phosphor. A phosphorescent substance which emits a detectable (visible) light when activated by ultra-violet light or similar electromagnetic radiation. The ink containing the phosphor is printed on the surface of the paper or the stamp, sometimes in bands or lines, sometimes all over. It is particularly provided for use with automatic letter facing and sorting machines. Phosphor lines are visible to the eye when the surface of the stamp is held at an angle to reflect a light source. Under an ultra-violet lamp the phosphor may give off different colour reactions which allow specialists to differentiate between printings of the same stamp.

For full details of the various phosphor-coated, phosphor-prepared papers collectors are referred to the "Connoisseur Catalogue of Machin Printings", and to "Stanley Gibbons' Great Britain Specialised Catalogue" volume four.

Stamps treated with phosphor (sometimes known as "tagged" issues) are produced by several countries and helecon and fluorescent papers have similar functions.

Photogravure (Photo). A widely used process of stamp printing. The negative plate is built up by photographic reproduction of the design in as many positions as there will be stamps on the sheet. This negative is then used, after processing through a screened carbon tissue, to create copper plates, on which the design to be printed is etched.

In photogravure printing a different plate is required for each colour to be used in the creation of the finished stamp, although half-tone effects can be achieved using a single colour.

Several distinct flaws or varieties can be created by this process depending on when in the plate creation sequence they occur. 1) With a flaw on a master negative, every stamp created from that master would also show that flaw. 2) With a flaw on a multipositive every stamp printed from plates created from that multipositive would show the same flaw at the same position on the sheet, which might involve an omission in the design or clear doubling caused by double exposure. 3) Gelatine or printing plate flaws would show on each stamp printed in that position on the sheets printed from that plate although other plates created from the same multipositive would not show these.

PHQ Cards. Special picture postcards issued by the Post Office where the pictures correspond with the designs of special or commemorative issues of stamps.

Pictorial. Literally stamps having a picture (rather than a portrait, symbol or coat of arms) as the design. The dividing line is somewhat obscure since many symbols are themselves pictorial. Pictorials come in most categories of stamps such as commemoratives and special issues. as well as *definitives*.

Picture Postcards (PPC). A postcard commercially produced having a picture or other design on one side and space on the reverse for the address. On early picture postcards the reverse was only to be used for the address, any message having to be written on the picture side. These are known as *undivided backs*. Later this regulation was modified and half the back could be used for the address and half for the message, it being divided across the centre by a line or other mark. These are known as *divided backs*. The pictures fall into many popular collecting categories such as art, transport, humour, patriotic, ethnic as well as the most common, views, and of course there have been many publishers. The cards themselves also may be categorised by the type of printing or visual effect such as *hold to light, fabs, magic effects, composite* etc. (see also *PHQ cards*).

Piece. Part of an envelope, cover or other postal wrapping on which the stamp and possibly the cancellation or other postal marking remain. They are very often retained in this form in order to display complete postmarks and other marks or *cachets*, or combinations of stamps, or to confirm official usage such as *bisected stamps* (although a complete cover would be preferable).

Pigeon Post. The use of pigeons for carrying messages has occurred from the earliest times. However on a number of occasions in recent times pigeons have been used to carry mail, the most notable being from beseiged Paris in 1870. Messages were originally written on the very flimsiest sheets of paper, but modern techniques allow the pigeon to carry messages on microfilm which is converted back into readable size print on arrival at its destination. Most recent pigeon posts have had some charity or publicity aspect rather than the provision of a necessary service.

Pillar Box. A box set up in a public place in which the public deposit letters for the post. Pillar boxes date from Paris in the 1650s, but they were not introduced to Britain until 1856, after Anthony Trollope, the novelist and Post Office surveyor, observed their use on a visit to the Channel Islands. Some countries used special cancellations to indicate the letter had been posted in a pillar box. There are many different designs including boxes made to be built into walls or to be affixed to posts.

Pillars. Various rectangular designs printed in the *gutter margins* between the panes on sheets of stamps. They were introduced to reduce wear on the printing plate and also to prevent unprinted watermarked paper falling into the hands of forgers.

Pinhole. A tiny defect in a stamp caused by a pin, staple or other sharp object, and through which light can be seen. It reduces the value of the stamp even though many are hardly noticeable, especially from the front.

Pin Perforation. A perforation created by sharp pointed pins which do not in fact remove any paper and make a hole rather than a cut.

Plain. Word used to describe an *ordinary* or untreated stamp from one with phosphor bands, fluorescent paper, etc.

Planography. A means of printing from a smooth surface whether flat bed or cylindrical, including collotyping, hectography, lithography (the most common), mimeography, etc.

Plate. The actual sheet of metal to which the ink is applied and from which stamps are printed, either directly or via an offset roller.

Plate Block. A term to indicate a block of stamps attached to that part of the sheet margin on which is printed the plate number (or Cylinder block for cylinder numbers).

Plate Number. Each plate will normally be engraved with a number, thus allowing sheets of stamps printed from it to be readily identified. In the case of many early Great Britain stamps the plate number was also incorporated as part of the stamp design. In more recent issues where a different plate is used for each colour all the plate (or cylinder) numbers will be printed close together in one part of the sheet margin (see *Cylinder number*).

Plate Variety. A variation in the design caused by a flaw or damage on the printing plate, or because the individual items on the plate have all been engraved separately.

Plate varieties are extremely helpful in determining the particular plate by which a stamp was printed and even the exact position on the plate.

Even wear and tear can be regarded as a plate variety when its progression enables a collector to define different printings, particularly if it shows in one significant feature of the design such as a frame line, etc.

Plebiscite Issues. Stamps produced in certain European areas whilst plebiscites (referenda) were held enabling the population to determine under which country's rule they wished to live.

Plug. A loose part of a printing plate such as the value or numeral which may be inserted or removed as required. This allowed several values to be printed from one plate.

Pneumatic Post. A means of carrying mail in special containers through (relatively) airtight tubes by the use of compressed air. In some instances it was purely for post office convenience: in others the public could use the service on prepayment of the appropriate fee. Some postal authorities issued special adhesives or letter cards for use on the service.

Poached Eggs. A popular name for special labels produced in order to test automatic vending machines.

Pochette. A small transparent pocket used in the 1930s for mounting mint stamps without the *hinge* damaging the gum. In practice many of them shrank slightly causing bending and buckling to the stamps therein. Their use has now been largely superceded by later developments in *mounts*.

Polyvinyl Alcohol (PVA). The gum now used by most postal administrations. As it is normally colourless, and relatively matt, a yellowish dye was often added. In 1973 it was introduced with dextrin added giving it a bluish tinge (and a better flavour?), the abbreviation for which is PVAD.

Pony Express. By the use of relays of pony riders the Pony Express service reduced to ten days, instead of about a month, the time taken for the mail to travel between St Joseph, Missouri and Sacramento, California in the USA in 1860. Discontinued following the completion of the telegraph link, Wells Fargo reintroduced it between San Francisco and Virginia City, Nevada, a year later.

Porous Paper. A description of very soft absorbent paper very susceptible to damp and thus not really suitable for high quality letterpress or litho printing.

Positional Piece. Any stamp or multiple with margins attached, the inscriptions or other markings on which allow its particular position on the sheet to be identified. Particularly useful for confirming the existence and location of constant varieties.

Postage Due. The amount of money due for collection on delivery of a letter or parcel because it has been posted without, or with insufficient, postage prepaid for the service or weight. Postage due labels are issued in order to collect and account for this fee which is normally charged at double the deficiency. Postage due labels are also used to collect customs and excise dues on dutiable items being imported through the post.

Items requiring postage due to be collected may carry a variety of handstamps, manuscript or other markings to indicate the fact. Of the more common is the letter "T" (French: taxe) and the amount as a fraction of the total which should have been paid.

Postal Currency. Treasury tokens accepted by the United States' Post Office in payment for stamps. Not to be confused with *currency stamps*.

Postal Fiscal. A fiscal or revenue stamp which has been authorised for use in the postal service.

Postal History. In the philatelic sense the study through the collecting of covers, entires, pieces and other documents of the development of the postal services within a particular country, state, city or town. Hence postal historians will tend not to be interested in single stamps unless the cancellation provides sufficient information as to their use and purpose. They will however pay considerable attention to manuscript markings, transit marks, special cancellations and *cachets* on covers which may indicate the rates charged, the route followed, the time taken etc. for the particular item in question. By relating this to earlier or later items they will build up a picture of how the post operated, how new routes developed and new services were introduced. By background reading they can set this against national events and industrial or cultural development.

Postally Used. The term used to describe a stamp which has been used to prepay postage (see *cancelled to order*).

Postal Rates. The tariff applying to the various categories and weights of mail. The Uniform Penny Postage rate remained unchanged for seventy-eight years following its introduction in 1840. Since 1918 however, the changes (usually increases) in the postal rates have occurred at ever more frequent intervals and now happen almost every year.

Postal Stationery. Items of stationery such as envelopes, postcards, air letters and newspaper wrappers which have been impressed with a stamp and which are sold at a price inclusive of the postage fee. Postal stationery predates by many years the adhesive postage stamp. The impressed stamp was very often cut out from the envelope or card and put into stamp collections. These "cut-outs" however are not much collected now since collectors prefer to collect the complete item with all the other printing on it and, if used, with the postal markings.

In recent times many postal authorities have produced very attractive ranges of illustrated postal stationery and collectors have not been slow to use these to introduce variety into collections or even start sideline collections. As with adhesive stamps, varieties and errors occur and these of course command premium prices.

Postal Telegraph. Telegraph stamp authorised either temporarily or permanently and used on a postal item. Such items are best collected on cover (or large piece) proving their postal usage since many telegraph and postal cancellations are very similar and sometimes indistinguishable.

Postbus. A service operating in rural and remote districts where a collection, franking and delivery facility is provided on the local bus. Sometimes the Post Office provides, in addition to the services mentioned, the bus service as well. Mail posted on such vehicles usually carries an identifying postmark or *cachet*.

Postcard Stamp. A stamp used purely for the prepayment of the postage fee on a postcard, either locally or nationally. This fee was generally lower than the normal postage fee for a letter. Some special stamps issued did not show the value of the fee but were merely inscribed to show the special use.

Postcode. A code added to the address to facilitate faster and more accurate sorting in the post office. Such codes may in some countries merely be a code for the town (usually four or five figures). Others, comprising a combination of letters and numerals, specifically identify a district, walk, street or even building or company. Known in the USA as the *Zip code*.

Postmark. Any mark applied to a postal item to record the date and place of posting. Such marks may be manuscript, handstruck or machine applied and may or may not actually cancel the postage stamp. Additional postmarks may indicate special routing, timings, transit and receipt details.

Many postmarks form part of the cancellation applied to the postage stamp either as part of a duplex, machine roller or slogan cancellation. It is important, however, to realise that whilst a cancellation is any defacing mark on a postage stamp it is not necessarily a postmark. Similarly an *obliterator* or *dumb cancel* is most definitely not a postmark since its purpose was only to deface the stamp.

Collectors and particularly postal historians depend upon the postmark on the letter or envelope to provide them with information concerning the journey through the post of that item. The postal authorities use postmarks to regulate and monitor the services they provide for their customers. An additional advantage of machine cancellors is the accurate quantitative information they can provide enabling post offices to deploy their manpower in the best way.

Postmaster's Stamps. Stamps produced locally by postmasters in order to collect postage fees. They were sometimes issued before supplies of an authorised national or government issue became available or sometimes during an emergency.

Post Office Mauritius. The name by which the 1847 (first) issue of Mauritius is known since both the Penny and Twopenny were wrongly engraved "Post Office" at the left instead of "Post Paid". The error was corrected on the second issue and as only about a dozen examples of each value of the "Post Office" are known it is one of the rarest and most valuable stamps.

Post Offices Abroad. Satellite post offices of one country located in another either by favour or by occupation. Such offices generally used overprinted, surcharged or inscribed stamps or had particular cancellors issued to them recognisable by letter, number or a combination of both.

Pre-Cancel. Stamps issued by postal authorities, usually to commercial organisations making large mailings, with a form of cancellation already printed on. This saves the Post Office having to cancel large quantities of mail emanating from one source. The pre-cancel inscription normally shows the place or state of issue, sometimes with a date or year. Collectors, apart from specialists, tend to shun such issues preferring stamps cancelled in the usual manner with a *circular date stamp*.

Presentation Pack. A special pack of stamps, made up and sold by the Post Office, usually containing a set of commemoratives or special issues together with the details of printing and design and other back-up information (see *year packs*).

Pre-Stamp. A cover, envelope, entire or other postal item used in a country before the issue of adhesive postage stamps in that country.

Primitive. A general term used to describe the early locally-produced issue of a country, particularly if the design and printing are of a variable quality. Primitives are very often known to collectors by popular names such as the "Sydney Views" of New South Wales, or the "Woodblocks" of the Cape of Good Hope.

Printed Both Sides. A stamp on which the design has been printed the correct way round but on both sides of the paper. Do not confuse with *offset* where the impression on the back is a mirror image of the design.

Printed On The Gummed Side. A stamp with a design printed on the back (usually by mistake) either underneath or sometimes on top of the gum. In the latter case the removal of the gum will remove the design.

Printer's Waste. Any partly printed sheets discarded by the printer, generally from set-up or preliminary runs. Also badly printed sheets subsequently rejected by the printer's quality control inspectors. All such material should be pulped, shredded or otherwise destroyed. However it does appear in the philatelic market masquerading as major errors when in fact, a true error so far as collectors are concerned should have been sold over the post office counter in the normal course of business.

Prisoner Of War Mail. A letter or other postal item to or from a prisoner of war, which usually bears some evidence such as a *cachet*, censor label or other mark to indicate this fact. Special postal stationery or local stamps have also been produced for use in these circumstances.

Private Perforation. Unofficial perforation of normally imperforate sheets made by companies or private individuals and even occasionally local postmasters.

Private Postage Stamp. Generally speaking another name for a *local stamp* although there have been one or two properly authorised private stamps used on a particular item or class of mail in the normal post.

Pro Aero. Stamps or overprinted stamps issued in Switzerland from time to time for use on special flights, the proceeds from the sale of which went into the Pro Aero Fund. They are similar to charity stamps in the fund raising aspect except that in many instances the stamp is compulsory on mail being carried on that particular flight.

Pro Juventute. Swiss charity stamps, the additional premium on which is donated to child welfare charities. Normally one set is issued each year. There have been many designs and they form a popular collecting category.

Proof. A sample printing made to determine the printing's quality. It is usually taken in black on a high quality card or paper. The sequence of proofs allows all parties involved in the production of the stamp to check that the design as it progresses is correct and up to the quality required. A *die proof*, once agreed, allows the engraver to pass the *master die* to the platemaker. A *plate proof* once agreed allows the platemaker to pass the plate to the printer. A colour proof once agreed allows the printer to proceed with the printing.

Propaganda. A stamp bearing some sort of message either specific or implied to promote a cause or country. These may fall into political, religious, commercial or promotional categories.

Pro Patria. Swiss charity stamps, the additional premium on which is donated to recognised national charities. Since 1952 one set inscribed "Pro Patria" has been issued each year. Earlier stamps with a similar purpose were inscribed "Fête Nationale".

Provisional. Stamps put into use during temporary shortages of the correct denominations or designations. Such stamps may be surcharged issues, issues of another country suitably overprinted, as for example where a name has changed or another ruler or system of government has been installed, or even specially designed locally produced issues such as the stamps produced in Mafeking during the siege of that town in the Boer War.

Publicity Cancel. A term generally used to describe a particular group of slogan cancels or *postmarks* where the town or region is advertised to attract either tourists or industrialists to visit it.

Pull Outs. Picture postcards having pictures printed in concertina fashion on lighter paper and which fold under the flap on the card but which pull out when opened.

Quadrillé. 1) Paper watermarked with a pattern of small squares or rectangles. 2) A term used to describe the small squares or grille printed on album leaves to assist with the layout of a collection.

Quarter. The quarter part of a stamp designed to be divided into four and used individually (see *splits*).

Quartz Lamp. A popular name for a lamp producing ultra-violet light. It is used by philatelists for determining printing inks, identifying phosphor and other fluorescent substances and also as an aid in the detection of repairs, thin spots, removed and cleaned cancellations etc.

Queen Enthroned. A popular name for various early issues from Victoria in contrast to the *Half lengths*.

Questa. More properly the House of Questa, a leading security printer of stamps.

Railway Post Office. Normally abbreviated to RPO on postmarks used on trains (see *Travelling post office*).

Railway Stamp. A stamp issued by railway companies against payment of the fee charged for the conveyance of a parcel or letter between railway stations. Such stamps were not valid in the general postal service and an item required to be forwarded on would require normal postage stamps in addition.

Rainbow Trials. Impressions of the Penny Black produced in a number of different colours during 1840. This was to test various combinations of coloured inks, papers and cancellations. They are easily recognisable because they lack the corner letters at the bottom, and the top right corner was blank.

Rarity. A term applied to indicate scarceness. Many of the world's rarities will never come onto the market since they are housed in national collections where they may be seen and enjoyed by countless collectors who would otherwise never see them. Others reside in some of the famous collections and change hands only infrequently, although they may be displayed at international exhibitions, again for the enjoyment and appreciation of collectors. Others are still to be discovered or rediscovered and this possibility adds the je ne sais quoi which every collector feels for their hobby.

Rawdon, Wright, Hatch and Edson. An American security printing firm which in 1858 amalgamated with six others to create the American Bank Note Company.

Rayon. A radial band distanced from a central point used to calculate and apply postage rates in Switzerland. The early Swiss stamps for each postage rate were inscribed Rayon I, Rayon II or Rayon III and are popularly knowns as "Rayons".

Recess Printing. The technique of printing where the ink is retained in the recesses of the printing plate before being transferred to the paper in the form of the design. Thus *line engraved*, *intaglio* and *photogravure* are all forms of recess printing.

Reconstruction. The assembling of stamps in their original positions to form the complete sheet. Also known as plating, although this tends to signify more the identifying of stamps to their particular plate.

Recorded Delivery. A postal service, on a national basis, whereby the delivery of the item will be occasioned by the giving of a signature by the recipient. Some compensation may be payable in the event of loss where proof of delivery cannot be established. An extra fee is levied by the use of normal postage stamps for items carried in this service which must also bear a recorded delivery *etiquette* with an identifying number (see *Registered mail*). It is particularly useful for formal documents which in themselves have no great value, or items of small value for which the registration fee would be out of proportion.

Recorded Message Stamp. In Argentina special stamps were issued in prepayment of extra postage fees on recorded discs containing messages sent through the post.

Re-Cut, Re-Engraved. A term used to indicate additional engraving has been effected on either the original die or the printing plate, usually to strengthen worn parts.

If the re-cutting is applied to the original die this may produce a recognisably different impression on subsequent printings from all plates made from the re-cut die. The dies might then be known as Die I and Die II, or some description to differentiate between them.

If the re-cutting is applied to the printing plate then this may produce recognisably different impressions in the printing after re-cutting, allowing philatelists to collect before and after specimens from the same sheet position (see *re-entry*).

Red Cross Stamp. 1) A stamp issued commemorating the Red Cross, its activities or anniversaries etc. 2) A charity stamp carrying a premium the proceeds from which will be donated to the Red Cross. These may also be commemoratives or merely surcharged general issues.

Redrawn. Indicates that the plate has been redrawn and a new master or mother die has been created, usually with easily recognisable differences from the original.

Re-Entry. Indicates that the plate has been re-entered or impressed a second time by the original die in order to strengthen the impression following wear and tear. If the second impression does not exactly coincide with the original impression or the original impression has not been fully eliminated, then this will show on the printed stamps as thickening or doubling of lines or other features. Such re-entries are known as non-coincident whilst those which coincide exactly and therefore merely show an overall strengthening of the design are known as coincidental. Philatelists recognise before and after specimens from the same position on the sheet.

Regional. A stamp issued in a particular region of a country and bearing some design or emblem appropriate to that region. Such stamps are, however, valid anywhere in the country concerned.

Registered Post. A postal service whereby special security handling is provided for the letter or parcel and on which if lost or damaged the Post Office will pay compensation up the value of the loss or within prescribed limits. A special registration fee is collected in addition to the normal postage and this fee varies according to the compensation level required. Some countries have issued special registration stamps to collect this fee, others merely use normal postage stamps. Under the Universal Postal Convention of Rome, 1906, all countries are required to identify registered mail by use of an adhesive registration label or *etiquette* which should show the origin and registration number of the item to which it is attached. Many countries also produce special registered postal stationery envelopes, the purchase price of which includes the standard rate of postage and the lowest fee. Such envelopes are recommended for the transference of cash.

Regular. Synonymous with ordinary and used in America to differentiate either *definitive* issues from *commemoratives,* or ordinary stamps from *tagged issues*.

Regummed. A descriptive term used by dealers and auctioneers to indicate a stamp from which the original gum has been removed and a new coat applied. This is usually done fraudulently in order to deceive collectors into paying more than the true value of the stamp in its original condition, sometimes by helping to disguise the fact that a stamp may have been used and has had the cancellation removed. It is usually recognisable since the colour, texture and appearance of the gum will differ from the original.

Reissue. A particular design of stamp which having once been withdrawn is put back into use either as it is or with a slight design, colour or currency modification.

Relief Printing. A printing process also known as surface printing or typography in which the ink is transferred from the raised surface of the printing plate to create the design (see *recess printing, lithography*).

Remainder. Bulk stocks of stamps which remain after an issue is withdrawn and which are subsequently sold off, usually at considerably reduced prices. Sometimes remainders are cancelled by some identifying means and collectors should beware of buying such stamps at exaggerated prices. Many catalogues indicate which issues have been remaindered and give some guide to any remainder cancellations which may have been applied. Excessive or uncontrolled remaindering inevitably affects the popularity of that country with collectors and most postal authorities recognise that it is better to destroy their remainder stocks rather than incur the displeasure of collectors and the resulting loss of revenue.

Repair. The correction of some flaw or damage to a printing plate or cylinder.

Repaired Impression. Refers to stamps printed after a plate has been repaired in order to differentiate them from stamps printed before the repair was made.

Repaired Stamp. An expression used by dealers and auctioneers to described a stamp on which a defect or fault has been repaired in order to enhance its value. Such repairs may involve adding paper or pulp to hide thins, increase margins etc.; colouring in rubbed parts of the design; adding perforations or corners from other stamps etc. (see *Cleaned, fakes, reperforated, regummed*).

Reperforated Stamp. A stamp which has had the perforations added either to an imperforated edge, a damaged margin or along a removed wing margin in order to defraud collectors.

Reply Coupons. See *International reply coupons*.

Reply Paid Card. A two-part postal stationery card in which both parts are impressed with a stamp, the second part of which may be detached and used for the reply without further postage fees being collected.

Repp Paper. A special paper with a corrugated surface of very fine lines which is usually soft and heavy. Also known as ribbed paper.

Reprint. 1) A further printing of a current stamp in the same colours and on the same paper as the original. Shade differences or sheet markings may enable collectors to distinguish them. 2) A printing from the original plate of a *demonetised* or withdrawn issue in similar colours to the original but usually easily recognisable by reason of shade, paper or watermark differences, etc. Official reprints may be made for record or souvenir purposes and their issue should be properly controlled and authenticated. 3) Unofficial reprints have been made by unscrupulous dealers who have acquired the printing plates either openly or clandestinely with the sole purpose of generating revenue from collectors. Many such reprints appear in old collections and in many cases are more common than originals, so much so that collectors assume every stamp of that issue or country they see to be a reprint unless expertised or certificated by an expert.

Reserve. A price set on an auction lot by the vendor below which the auctioneer may not sell that particular lot. Many auctioneers also determine a starting price for a lot which in effect becomes an unofficial reserve, although the auctioneers will exercise their discretion to accept or reject bids received below this level. They may not do so on an official reserve without reference back to the vendor.

Resinised Paper. Sometimes known as "Goldbeater's Skin", it is paper rendered transparent by saturation in resin.

Retouch. Now mostly refers to minor corrections of flaws, made directly on to the cylinder in photogravure printing.

Returned Letter. A letter returned to the sender usually because the Post Office has been unable to deliver it to the addressee; sometimes because it has been underfranked or is in some other way unacceptable to the Post Office. Such letters usually bear handstamps or manuscript marks to indicate the reason for return. In some instances a return postage fee will be collected by means of *postage due* labels.

Revenue Stamp. A fiscal stamp used for collecting tax or duties other than postal or telegraph fees.

Reversed. 1) A watermark which though the right way up only reads correctly when seen from the back of the stamp. It implies that the stamp has been printed on the wrong side of the paper. 2) A part of the design or inscription on a stamp or overprint which is back to front (i.e. a mirror image) compared with the correct design. 3) A printer's term indicating that the letter, numerals or specific part of the design is left white (usually) and is therefore said to be reversed out of the darker colour surrounding it.

Reward Card. A picture postcard awarded to a pupil for merit for various education authorities and some other organisations.

Ribbed Gum. Gummed paper tends to curl and therefore certain stamps have been printed with the gum applied in narrow parallel bands in order to counteract this curling tendency.

Rice Paper. A very thin paper which has been sized with rice water.

Rocket Mail. Covers or cards transmitted between two places by rockets and bearing evidence of this fact. No official rocket mail has ever provided a regular service. Most envelopes or cards carried on rockets have been of an experimental, publicity, charity or purely speculative nature. Several attempts to link islands have generally not been successful. Mail carried in rockets has required the addition of normal postage stamps before it was further transmitted in the postal service and apart from one or two exceptions any special "rocket" stamps have been privately produced.

Roll. A complete coil of stamps. *Coil stamps* are known as roll stamps in some countries and catalogues. The roll may be produced either for use in automatic vending machines or for the use of companies using large quantities of a single denomination.

Roll Of Distinguished Philatelists. A scroll which distinguished philatelists are invited to sign following proposal to and election by the Philatelic Congress of Great Britain. It was instituted in 1921, the first signatory being King George V. A signing ceremony now takes place each year during congress week.

Roman. A typeface whose letters are upright, as opposted to slanting.

Roos. A popular abbreviated name for the issues of Australia which showed a kangaroo in the centre of a map of the country.

Rotary. 1) Perforation in which the sheet passes between two rotating wheels, one having holes and the other flat ended pins, which marry exactly with each other thus punching holes in the paper. 2) A printing process where the plate is fixed to a rotating cylinder and where the paper, passing round another cylinder, is put in contact either with the printing plate directly or with the *offset* rubber roller.

Rotogravure. *Gravure* or *photogravure* printing.

Rough Perf. Perforation in which, due to wear and tear or poor alignment of the perforating pins, the paper which the perforator should cut out remains partly joined to the stamp, or if pulled away leaves a rough edge to the hole (see *Clean perforation*).

Roulette. The small cuts or holes made at regular intervals in the paper between stamps in order to assist in separation. Unlike perforation no paper is removed in rouletting. There are various patterns of knife cut: simple short straight cuts in straight lines: cuts at angles to one another, cuts in the shape of crosses, etc. Each one produces a different shape to the teeth at the edge of the stamp after separation (see *Percé*).

Row. One horizontal line of stamps running across the sheet, as compared with a column which is similar but runs vertically up and down the sheet.

Royal Certificate. Certificate of authenticity or otherwise issued by an expert committee of the Royal Philatelic Society of London.

Royal Collection. The collection of stamps and other philatelic items now belonging to Her Majesty Queen Elizabeth II and which was originally started by Prince George (later to become King George V) and added to by King George VI. Items from it are regularly displayed in the Queen's Gallery at Buckingham Palace and at major philatelic exhibitions. Traditionally a display from the Royal Collection is presented to members of the Royal Philatelic Society of London at their first meeting each season.

Royal Cypher. The monarch's initials, sometimes including the appropriate number in addition together with the letter "R" (signifying Rex or Regina). For example, GVR indicates King George V and GVIR King George VI.

When used on watermarks of British and British Commonwealth stamps it may further be described as simple, multiple or block etc.

It has also been used as an inscription on stamps generally in the form of a *paraph*.

Royal Philatelic Society of London. Popularly known as the "Royal" it was originally founded in 1869 receiving royal recognition in 1906. It holds regular meetings in London, has an extensive philatelic library, together with a collection of early stamp production items such as plates and dies. It provides a certification facility using the services of many acknowledged authorities on its expert committees. The *Royal Certificate* is recognised throughout the world as an authoritative document of the genuiness or otherwise of the item for which it is issued. The society also sponsors stamp exhibitions and publishes reference books. The *London Philatelist* is its official journal. The initials RPSL are used to signify membership.

Rub (or Rubbed). Descriptive of surface damage to a stamp caused by rubbing against rough or abrasive surfaces usually while in transit. It reduces the value of the stamp.

Run. Descriptive of fugitive ink which has come into contact with water causing it to diffuse or run into the paper, generally losing or changing colour. Fugitive inks, particularly greens and purples, were used extensively on Victorian and Edwardian issues, the original dull green, for example, turning pale yellow green when coming into contact with water. Stamps having ink which has run are reduced in value and sometimes described as shot.

Rust, Rusting. See *Foxed*.

Safety Paper. Paper which is safe in the sense that it has been treated to prevent the fraudulent removal of the cancellation or impression. Various methods may be used such as coating the paper with a chemical or varnish before printing, or printing *Burélage* upon it. The most commonly used safety paper is *chalk-surfaced paper*.

Said To Catalogue (STC). Most often found as the abbreviation used by auctioneers. It means that the catalogue value quoted has been supplied by the vendor and has not been checked in detail. However whilst the bidder will consider it when determining his bid he should remember that the auctioneer will have set his estimate after looking at the lot, based on a number of other factors such as condition, completeness, quantity etc. as well as the information supplied by the vendor.

Saint Andrew's Cross. The name given to the diagonal cross design printed on the otherwise blank label in a pane of booklet stamps issued during King Edward VII's reign in Great Britain. Also used by Austria where the design and layout of the sheet in relation to the paper would leave white space available to a forger. Also known as the "Kiss" print.

Saint Edward's Crown Watermark. A watermark used on Queen Elizabeth II stamps of Great Britain which incorporates a representation of the Saint Edward's Crown alternating with the royal cypher (see *Tudor Crown*).

Saints. Collective word for the islands in the British West Indies which form a popular collecting group. St. Christopher, St. Kitts, St. Lucia, St. Vincent (and sometimes St. Helena, although this is not in the West Indies).

Sans Serif. A printer's term to describe a typeface having no serifs (i.e. cross strokes) at the end of each stroke on the individual letters.

Saw Tooth Roulette. English translation of *percé en scie*.

Schermack Perforation. Perforations made by the Schermack Mailing Machine Company on USA stamps between 1906 and 1923. They were used mainly for producing coil stamps and collectors recognise three distinct types including one consisting only of two slits punched in the vertical margins between individual stamps.

Scinde Dawk. A popular name for the first stamp issued in India in 1852.

Scott. Reference to "Scott's Standard Postage Stamp Catalogue" published annually in USA by the company of the same name.

Screening. The process by which a *half-tone* picture or photograph is projected through a mesh screen. In doing so it is broken up into a series of small dots thus enabling the half-tone effect to be created by the printing plate even though only one shade of ink is used.

Script. A typeface which looks like handwriting. It is not often used on stamps but frequently found in watermarks including that used by the *Crown Agents* for British Colonies' issues during the period 1927 to 1957, known as multiple script CA.

Seahorse. A popular name for the high value stamps of Great Britain issued during the reign of King George V.

Secret Marks. Tiny design features sometimes undetectable except with a glass and an idea of where to look. The object was to identify the engraver or a change of plate and also to allow the Post Office to detect forgeries. Very often they were initials but also on occasion dots or dashes or other embellishments (see *Hidden dates*).

Security Endorsement. *Overprint, underprint* or *perfin* by which means commercial companies or government departments seek to prevent the use of their stamps by their employees on private mail (see *Chop*.)

Security Paper. See *safety paper*.

Self-Adhesive. Some stamps use self adhesive gum, that is a gum which does not need the application of water (or a lick) to make it stick. These stamps are produced with a peelable backing sheet which is removed when the stamp is required for use.

Self-adhesive stamps are difficult to remove from envelopes and most collectors therefore collect such stamps on small pieces. Some self-adhesive gum is removable with a spirit such as lighter fuel but the process is both laborious and risky.

Selvedge. 1) The unprinted margins of a sheet of stamps. Collectors at one time used small pieces of these to mount stamps in their albums. Many mint stamps have been ruined by this since the piece of selvedge is almost impossible to remove without damaging the gum on the stamp. 2) The extra piece of margin by which a *pane* of stamps is stitched or stapled into a booklet and remains behind when the stamps are detached.

Semi-Official. Issues not fully authorised by the Post Office, usually made by rail or air companies but on which *postage due* was not collected. In some instances the Post Office acted as agent. The stamps were restricted to a particular use such as the Condor flights in Brazil or the Great Western Rail–Air Service in Great Britain.

Serpentine Roulette. A roulette which leaves very pronounced teeth on the stamp edge similar to the humps of a serpent. Also known as *Percé en serpentine* .

Service mail. Mail bearing evidence of being sent to or from a serviceman on active duty. Such mail was very often carried postage free, although probably subject to censorship. Sometimes stamps specially overprinted with the initials of the force in question would be available for use on this mail (see *Field Post Office*).

Set. A collective noun used to describe a group of stamps which form a collecting unit, generally issued on the same day on the same theme. In the case of *definitives* a set may be issued over a period of time as new values and colours are added. Longer sets may be advertised and sold as complete sets or as short sets which will comprise all the lower values up to the value specified. An *omnibus set* refers to the stamps issued at the same time in different countries to commemorate the same event or theme and having similar designs.

Set To. A term used by dealers and auctioneers to indicate that the set on offer is complete up to the value indicated including major changes of colour but not shade or perforation varieties. Sometimes the adjective "basic" is used to indicate that rare printings are specifically not included (see *Values to*).

Se-Tenant. Any multiple comprising stamps of different varieties, usually different face values or designs. Many booklet *panes* and miniature sheets have stamps se-tenant in their make-up and such items are produced from sheets specially printed for the purpose. However other varieties occur se-tenant due to errors of the platemakers or printers in making up plates or because of repairs or damage to the plate during printing. Such varieties are described as se-tenant when attached to a stamp printed correctly (see *tête bêche*).

Set Off. Ink transferred during or after printing from one sheet to the back of another and which shows the design in mirror image (see *Off-set*).

Setting. A printing term to describe the exact layout of loose type as "set" or laid out by the compositor and made up into a plate. Differences between the actual typeface used, the line length, spaces between words or lines, or the relative positions of words or letters enable collectors to recognise different settings of an overprint of or surcharge.

Sewing Machine Perforation. Perforation produced on a sewing machine. Since a needle is used rather than a pin the effect looks more like *rouletting* or very rough perforation.

Shade. The precise colour of a stamp, but used in philatelic circles to indicate a variation from the basic colour which may occur between different printings, providing such variation is not sufficient to change the colour. Thus red and orange are different colours but orange-red or reddish-orange might be considered shades of the red and orange depending upon the degree of difference. Stricty speaking the terms light and dark are hues of the same colour but are also commonly referred to as different shades as are the adjectives bright and dull.

The eye can recognise and distinguish an infinite number of shades and colours but as stamps are prone to change colour under certain conditions or because of fading, collectors try to stick with the more easily definable ones.

Colour charts are available to assist collectors but these nearly always fail either because they are printed in solid colour whereas the colour on stamps is broken up by the design, or because traditional colour names describing classic stamps bear little or no resemblance to their modern colour equivalents.

Sheets. The largest layout of stamps issued by the Post Office on a single piece of paper. A sheet may comprise several *panes*, normally two or four but sometimes more, and the make-up will vary according to the size of the stamp and the printing method and machine used. Most modern sheets in countries where decimal coinage is in use will be in multiples of one hundred impressions but in earlier times quantities and shapes were many and varied.

Sheet Number. A number allocated in numerical sequence to each sheet after it is printed and usually to be found in the sheet margin. Used primarily for accounting and recording purposes, the sheet number is sometimes of interest to philatelists in determining the progression of damage or other variety to a plate (see *plate* and *cylinder numbers*).

Sheet Watermark. A watermark which appears only once in the sheet and which very often results in many stamps on the sheet having no watermark. Many *papermakers' watermarks* were in this form.

Ship Letter. Letters carried on board ships were postmarked "Ship Letter" when handed to the postal authorities at the arrival port (see *Packet mail*). Many such letters and covers also bear some indication of the name of the vessel or the routing followed and, with clear dates, provide historians with first class evidence of the development of shipping.

Short Perf. Term used to indicate that one (or more) of the perforation teeth on the stamp is missing, or shorter than the rest. This may have occurred when the stamp was separated from the sheet due to poor perforation or later due to carelessness or ignorance. In either case the value will be less than a stamp with full peforations though how much will depend on whether stamps of the issue are normally found with full perfs or if short perfs are the norm (see *Nibbed perf*).

Short Set. Set including all values and major colour changes up to the value indicated.

Short Stamp. Stamp on which the perforations on two parallel sides are closer together than usual. This may be because of the method of perforation (the stamp of the top row on some early sheets for example) or because the stamp has been *reperforated* in order to remove a defect.

Shrinkage. 1) Many types of paper, after being made wet, shrink unevenly when drying. Even different batches of the same paper may also shrink differently. Thus when a stamp has been printed by a method requiring the paper to be dampened, it will tend to vary however minutely from other stamps printed from the same plate. 2) Term used in the retail trade to describe stock losses attributed to shop lifting or staff pilferage.

Side Delivery. Coil or roll stamps, dispensed by the machine, joined at the sides instead of the top and bottom.

Sideways Watermark. A watermark which is sideways on to the design of the stamp. Many stamps are printed correctly (normally) with the watermark sideways, as for example coil stamps or booklet stamps, and stamps in the same set, where both horizontal and vertical designs occur for printing on the same paper. Sideways watermarks can also occur as a result of printing errors when the paper is put into the press in the wrong direction, the error perhaps only occurring on a few sheets. Sideways watermarks may also be found inverted or reversed when compared with the normal direction.

Seige Posts. Postal services set up between beseiged cities and the outside world. Covers are usually identifiable by special postmarks or *cachets*, or perhaps by the dates (see *Balloon post, pigeon post*).

Signé. A term used to indicate that the stamp has an *expertising* mark or signature on the back.

Silk Thread Paper. Paper having parallel silk threads running through it (see *Dickinson paper*).

Single, Singleton. A term for one stamp or used in the plural to contrast several individual stamps from a multiple (see *Copy, specimen*).

Sinking Fund Stamp. French postage stamp, the premium on which was used to reduce the national debt. Recognisably inscribed or overprinted "CA" or "Caisse D' Amortissement", their use was discontinued after only seven issues within about five years.

Slogan Cancellation. A postmark or cancellation, part of which carries a message (the slogan), generally machine applied. Slogans serve many purposes. Post Offices make considerable use of them in exhorting the general public to "Post early for Xmas" to "Use the postcode". Governments make use of them to boost morale or promote National Savings Certificates, Defence Bonds etc. Towns and cities make use of them for publicity purposes as do charities, commercial and other organisations, not least being philatelic and other local societies. Many collectors make extensive collections of slogan cancellations, usually on small pieces including the stamp and date stamp, but for general stamp collections, collectors prefer stamps having the *circular date stamp* rather than the slogan (see *Publicity cancellations*).

Smiling Boys. A popular name for the pair of *health stamps* issued by New Zealand in 1931.

Society. An organisation to which collectors may belong which usually meets at regular intervals for display and social purposes. By far the vast majority of members are members of local societies: others are members of national or special interest societies. They provide a forum in which collectors can meet, buy and sell stamps, display their own collections or see other collectors' displays, and generally exchange information and keep up to date with their hobby.

Soldier's Letter. See *service mail*.

Somerset House, London. 1) The department responsible until 1915 for the production of postage stamps in the United Kingdom, the Board of Inland Revenue, had its headquarters here. Thus it was: 2) The repository for the *imprimatur sheets* produced for registration purposes prior to the main printing. 3) Several issues of stamps have been printed at Somerset House, including the embossed stamps of 1847 and some printings of Edward VII and George V. 4) All British stamps and many colonial issues were perforated at Somerset House prior to 1930.

Souvenir Sheet. A miniature sheet, not necessarily postally valid, issued to commemorate a particular event such as a philatelic exhibition.

Sower. A popular name for the design on French stamps issued between 1903 and 1936 showing the figure of a female sower.

Space Filler. A defective or poor specimen of a valuable, rare or elusive stamp, sold at a small fraction of its catalogue price. It is used to fill the space in the album until a better copy can be found. The expression "attractive spacefiller" is sometimes used to indicate that the stamp looks fine from the front but will be severely defective at the back with thins or repairs, etc.

Spandrel. An approximately triangular surface bounded by the outer curve of an arch and the adjacent wall or horizontal cornice. Thus on stamps, that part of the design between the outside of the central portrait or oval and the outer frame line.

Special Delivery. A fast delivery service provided by many postal authorities on payment of the appropriate fee. Some countries issue special delivery stamps to collect the fee whilst others use ordinary postage stamps and identify the item by the use of special delivery etiquettes or *cachets* (see *express*).

Special Event Postmark. A machine slogan cancel, special handstamp or *cachet* publicising a particular event. These usually relate to exhibitions, shows or conferences and the application of the postmark is usually restricted to mail posted within the confines of the event at the temporary post office provided.

Special Handling. 1) A stamp issued in the USA the use of which upgraded the service in which the items of mail would be carried. 2) Labels provided by some postal authorities for use by philatelists to ensure that philatelic items are dealt with carefully, i.e. clear postmarks in the right position.

Specimen. 1) Under the rules of the Universal Postal Union all issues of stamps produced by its members must be circulated via its offices to all other members. Such stamps are normally overprinted or perfined "Specimen" (or the local equivalent) and used by the recipient country for reference purposes. 2) Sample stamps usually overprinted "Specimen" distributed gratis via the philatelic press or to influential people or organisations in the trade. 3) A single stamp may also be described as "a damaged specimen", a "fine specimen", "only one specimen seen" etc. and here the word is synonymous with "copy" or "stamp".

Speculative Stamps. In philatelic terms stamps which are deliberately issued in such as way as to create high prices for them when bought or resold, or issued with little postal need, merely to be sold to collectors. Many catalogues now refuse to price these latter items. Collectors are quick to recognise speculative issues and adapt their collecting interests accordingly. Because of this not all speculators make money out of their activities.

Split Stamps. Stamps authorised for and used as *bisects* or *quarters* sometimes having been surcharged and perforated for the purpose.

Spoon Cancellation. A popular name for a duplex handstamp where the two parts of the cancel overlap. The outline shape thus appears spoon-shaped. They were of an experimental nature and stamps or covers on which they have been used generally rate a premium by collectors. The one in use at Rugby is known as the "Rugby Shoe" because of its shape.

Spray Watermark. A popular name for the watermark resembling a single five petal "rose" used on Great Britain stamps between 1867 and 1880.

Stamp Duty. An inscription which usually indicates that the stamp is for use for fiscal or revenue purposes only. However various fiscal stamps have been authorised for postage. In the Australian state of Victoria during the period 1881–1899 all stamps were authorised for either postage or fiscal use and it was decreed that all stamps would bear the inscription "Stamp Duty".

Stampless. A term used to indicate a cover used after the introduction of adhesive stamps in that county but which does not have an adhesive. It will normally bear a postmark or other mark indicating the reason why no stamp has been used, or otherwise indicate that the postage fee has been paid (see *Pre-stamp*).

Stanley Gibbons (SG). The famous London and international stamp dealers, auctioneers and publishers. Their catalogues are recognised worldwide and dealers and auctioneers are allowed to quote Gibbons' catalogue numbers in advertisements lists and auction descriptions providing such numbers are preceded by the letters "SG".

Stars. 1) Watermarks in the shape of a star have been used in many countries. They may be variously described as small, large, broad, truncated, single, multiple, etc. Sideways or inverted watermarks can very often be determined by the position of the points in relation to the design of the stamp. 2) A popular name for the early engraved ornaments placed in the corner boxes of many early and primitive stamps. Variations in the exact pattern printed are of great help to specialists in identifying stamps from different plates and the position on the plates, as well as forgeries etc. 3) A popular name for the Great Britain Penny Red perforated issues in which the top corner squares contained ornaments sometimes referred to as "Union Jacks" but which looked more like stars, issued between 1854 and 1857.

Stated To Catalogue. See *Said to catalogue*.

Stereotype. A method of producing cast metal printing plates from a mould made from a forme of type matter, in papier-mâché or some other material.

Stock Book (S/B). A bound or loose leaf book containing leaves on which pockets have been provided by means of strips of cellophane, glassine or other material laid across the page at regular intervals and suitably secured. It is used to store loose stamps. The space between facing pages is usually inter-leaved with a sheet of cellophane to prevent the stamps on opposite pages catching on one another when the book is closed.

Stock Card (S/C). A single card or sheet having pockets similar to a stock book, which may be single or double sided.

Stock Exchange Forgery. A famous forgery of the Great Britain Queen Victoria One Shilling Green which was extensively used in the Stock Exchange and whose existance was not discovered until many years later. The forger was never identified.

Stone. Another word for the printing plate used on some early primitive issues.

Straight Edge. A term used to describe the edge of a wing margin stamp where the wing margin has been trimmed off. Also used for a stamp from the edge of a sheet where the outside edge is not perforated. Strictly speaking this is more correctly described as imperforate top, side or bottom as appropriate.

Straight Line. Descriptive of a handstamp or postmark in which the text is printed in one straight line.

Strike. The application of a cancellation or postmark to a cover. It is used in a descriptive expression such as "having a good strike" meaning a good clear impression of the postmark or handstamp.

Strike Stamp. A stamp issued by a private organisation to prepay fees on letters carried by them when the Post Office has been unable to offer a service due to its employees being on strike. This has happened in USA, France, Austria, Canada and Great Britain. Usually the strike stamps require the authority of the Postmaster General before being put into use and are very collectable if genuinely used, especially on cover. However, many strike stamps which came onto the market after the postal strike in 1971 in Great Britain did so as remainders, and in some instances it is not certain that genuinely used examples exist.

Strip. Three or more stamps from the same row (horizontal strip) or column (vertical strip) which are still joined together. A coil strip indicates that the stamps have come from a *coil* and a marginal strip indicates that the margin is attached along all stamps in the strip. The term gutter strip is used to describe strips of stamps joined by the *gutter margin* in between.

Submarine Post. Postal service operating during wartime using submarines. In some instances special stamps, ordinary stamps specially overprinted, or postal stationery were used; in others only the postmark can determine that the service was used.

Substitute Cliché. A block inserted into a plate to replace a damaged one (see *cliché*).

Suez Canal Stamps. Stamps issued during July and August 1868 by the Suez Canal Company (Compagnie Universelle du Canal Maritime de Suez) for use on their employees' mail. Although very collectable many forgeries exist.

Sulphuretted. Synonymous with *oxidised*.

Sunday Delivery. Stamp. Special stamp used for mail which was required to be delivered on a Sunday (see *Dominical labels*).

Surcharge. An overprint which may alter (up or down) or confirm the face value of the stamp. Also used sometimes when a new currency is introduced to use up stocks of stamps of the previous currency. Surcharges tend to be provisional issues required because existing stocks have run low, postage rates have been altered without adequate warning, or military or political changes have occurred. They are also used on occasions to raise money for charities or disaster funds etc.

As with all overprints, errors of surcharge such as inverted or double surcharges occur. Also settings may vary and in one or two cases the surcharges have been made in manuscript.

Surface Printing. Another name for typography or letter press printing in which the design to be printed is raised above the surface of the plate and the ink is applied to the raised surfaces, usually by roller.

Sydney Views. A popular name for the first issues of New South Wales which are supposed to depict an early view of settlement taken from the Great Seal of the Colony.

Tab. A small label or coupon in pair with a stamp, usually at the bottom. Tabs very often give descriptive details about the commemorative event or the stamp they adjoin. They have also been used (as *Dominical labels* for example) to give instruction either to the public or the Post Office, or as advertisements. In this latter case they are generally printed as part of the sheet margin or booklet *pane*. In all cases they should be collected still joined to the adjacent stamp.

Tablet. 1) A term sometimes used to describe the part of the inscription on a stamp containing the value (tablet). 2) A popular name for a stamp used for French Colonies very similar to the *Peace and Commerce* type of France and designed by M. E. Mouchon. In the tablet type the figures are said to represent commerce and navigation.

Tagged Issue. Stamps having a substance such as phosphor or Helecon printed on the paper or the stamp either as bands or all over. These substances activate the automatic letter facing and sorting machines in use in various countries (see also *Phosphor, Fluorescence*).

Target Cancel. Description of a cancellor made up of concentric circles which sometimes has a number or letter in the centre. It looks like a target.

Tear. A separation across the paper of a stamp caused by careless handling thereby making the stamp defective. Torn stamps are worth less than sound copies. A very small tear may be described as a nick or tiny nick. The term closed tear indicates that the edges of the tear match up and no part of the stamp is loose, i.e. separated from the other part. Closed tears are very often hidden by hinges or the addition of spurious backing paper but will normally show under a quartz lamp, if not visible to the naked eye by holding the stamp up to the light (see *mutilation*).

Telegraph Cancellation. Cancellation indicating that the stamp has been used to prepay telegraph fees. They have a *circular date stamp* which is very often difficult to distinguish from a postal circular date stamp, if only a small part remains on the stamp. Ordinary postage stamps were very often used to collect telegraph fees.

Telegraph Stamp. A special stamp issued to prepay the fee on a telegram or telegraph. In many countries telegraph stamps were issued by private companies until they were amalgamated with government services or nationalised. Official government designs were very often similar to postage stamps but inscribed "Telegraph" and in some cases were postage stamps overprinted "T.F.", etc.

Telephone Stamp. Stamps issued mainly by private telephone companies to confirm payment of the fees for telephone calls.

Testing Label. A stamp-sized label or sometimes specially cancelled stamps used for testing purposes with automatic vending machines (see *Poached egg*).

Tête Bêche. A pair of stamps one having the complete design inverted when compared with the other. This may have happened deliberately, as with the printing of sheets of stamps for making up into booklets, or accidently because of an error in making up the printing plate. The expression tête bêche applies equally to both horizontal or vertical pairs and also to stamps separated by a gutter margin.

Thematics. 1) The collection of stamps from different countries which have similar themes in their design or purpose, or which commemorate similar events or themes. Popular themes include illustrations on stamps of trains, butterflies or art; or stamps relating to scouts and scouting events, olympics, the Red Cross, music, chess, etc.

Handbooks or catalogues are produced on many themes or subjects providing collectors with information about the subject and a check list of relevant stamps. Perhaps one of the best known is the "Sanabria Catalogue of Airmails" which is a vast field. 2) Stamps whose design or purpose enables the collector to include them in a thematic collection.

Also known as topics or topical collecting.

Thermography, Thermoplastic. A special form of printing similar in principle to litho but in which the design is built up on the surface of the paper because of special ingredients in the ink which are heat treated. Unlike recess printing there is no complimentary distortion of the surface at the back of the stamp corresponding to the printed design on the front. Advances in thermography and other thermoplastic techniques have moved rapidly in recent years and more stamps are likely to be produced by these methods in the future.

Thin or Thinned. Describes a stamp in which some part of the surface of the paper at the back has been removed thus leaving the stamp thinner at that point. Usually thins are clearly visible as lighter spots when the stamp is held up to the light, or darker spots when placed in a watermark detector tray. Clever repairs are sometimes attempted but they are revealed if the stamp is put under a quartz lamp. Thinning reduces the value of a stamp.

Thirkell. The Thirkell Position Finder, a special grid used for identifying the location of flaws and varieties in a standard manner.

Tied. An expression used by philatelists to indicate that the postmark or cancel extends beyond the stamp onto the envelope or paper to which it is attached. This therefore confirms that the stamp is still on the original cover (or piece of it) for which it was postally used, unless of course the postmark itself is forged.

It is worth noting that unsurcharged *bisects* can only be verified as used if the cancel not only ties the stamp to the cover or piece but does so across the cut side or diagonal.

Tin Can Mail. 1) Letters set afloat in tin cans, or specially designed containers by residents of St. Kilda and allowed to float with the prevailing tide to the mainland. 2) Letters in special tin-can containers carried out to the monthly steamer by swimmers from the Tongan island of Niuafo'ou.

Tinsel. Used to add glitter to picture postcards for decorative effect.

Tinted. A papermakers' and printers' term to indicate a coloured paper as delivered from the mill. Not to be confused with a paper which has been printed all over with a coloured ink.

Toned. 1)Descriptive of the paper used in the printing of some stamps which has a brownish tinge. The full description "toned paper" should be used for such items to avoid confusion with (2). 2) Discolouration to the gum or paper of a stamp usually caused because it has been stored in unsuitable conditions. Depending upon the degree it will reduce the value of the stamp concerned (see *Foxing, Rusting, Tropicalisation*).

Tongs. See *Tweezers*.

Too Late Stamp. Same as *late fee stamp*

To Pay. The inscription of modern *postage dues* of Great Britain which are also used to collect import duties.

Topics. See *Thematics*.

Topographical. A picture postcard which illustrates local scenery, more commonly known as a view card. The category also includes cards which show buildings and monuments, churches, castles and other historical sites, street scenes, etc.

Toughra. The name given to a particular *paraph* used on early Turkish stamps, which was the symbol or signature of the sultan.

Town Stamp. Any postmark which includes the name of the town. The term normally applies to pre-stamp items and would include all the various shapes, straight line and boxed cancels. The term town cancel or town circle would more correctly describe similar marks on letters with adhesive stamps eventually culminating in the modern *circular date stamp*.

Tourism. A popular thematic area. Many countries have issued stamps illustrating their tourist attractions and facilities, very often in conjunction with suitable *publicity cancels*.

Traffic Light. A popular name for the large coloured dots printed in the sheet margins of modern stamps in the colours of the cylinders in use. They normally fall into a box provided where they resemble traffic lights. They are used for electronic and visual positioning, and checking to ensure the printing is correct.

Training Stamp. A stamp similar to a normal stamp used in the training of post office counter clerks.

Transfer. Most plate-making processes at some stage or other require the transfer of the original engraving or design to the printing plate either directly or indirectly. This action is known as tranferring. In recess printing it will be from the *master die* to the special roller (known as the transfer roller) which is used in turn to transfer the design to the plate as many times as there will be impressions on the sheet.

In litho printing the transfer may be via a paper or photographic transfer process. In either case any flaws which occur on the transfer medium will be reproduced on the printed stamps and are known as transfer flaws. If the master die is used to produce more than one transfer roller then each transfer roller may in turn produce different though constant flaws on the printing plates produced from it as compared with plates produced by other rollers. Terms such as transfer flaws, double transfer, creased or damaged transfer are used to describe such flaws according to how they have occurred.

Transit Marks. Postmarks which a letter or postal item receives on its journey through the post, charting its progress. The cancellation of the despatch office and the arrival *circular date stamp* of the receiving office, although not strictly transit marks, may indicate the two ends of the journey. Transit marks may indicate special routing, highlight delays and the reasons thereof, and would also include redirection marks and marks of the sorting offices through which the item passed.

Travelling Post Office (TPO). This abbreviation found in a postmark indicates that the item was sorted and cancelled on a travelling sorting office such as a train.

Triangular. Stamps printed in triangular shape, the most famous of which are the *Cape Triangulars*.

Trident. An overprint in the form of the trident (three pronged fork) found on Austrian and Russian stamps for use in the Ukraine.

Trimmed. 1) Describes stamps on which the perforations have been carelessly cut short along one or more sides during production. It almost entirely applies to coil and booklet stamps since these must be guillotined in the production process to make up the rolls or booklets. The extent of the trimming tends to reduce the value proportionately and in many cases where trimmed perforations tend to be the norm, a stamp having full peforations will command a considerable premium. 2) An expression sometimes used to describe a stamp which has been carelessly cut along some or all of the perforations on one or more sides. Also particularly a perforated stamp from which the perforations have been removed in order to pass it off as an imperforate copy, more correctly termed cut-down.

Triptych. A term describing a strip of three stamps with different designs *se-tenant,* the whole forming one design made up of three panels. They are best collected in units made up in the correct order and usually illustrate a well known art or religious theme.

Tropicalisation. Indicates that the condition of the stamp (particularly the gum) has been adversely affected by the climatic conditions. Usually because of the humidity and heat the colour may have run or the gum may have become discoloured or absorbed into the watermark part of the paper. Stamps affected are of less value than perfect specimens.

Tudor Watermark. 1) Tudor Crown watermark: the name given to the first watermark used for the Wilding *definitives* of Great Britain in which the crown design is representative of a Tudor crown (see *St. Edward's Crown*).

Tweezers. Special instruments used by collectors for handling stamps. The ends are flat and should have no sharp points or corners. Various types are popular such as spade-ends and rounded-ends and sometimes the arms are angled. Usually tweezers are chromium or nickel plated. By using tweezers collectors avoid transfering dirt or sweat from their fingers to the stamp and in fact the stamps are much more easily handled with tweezers than clumsy fingers. Collectors become very dependent upon their tweezers, sometimes keeping the same pair almost through their entire collecting life.

Twelve Pence Black. Always refers to the twelvepence stamp of Canada issued in 1851.

Typeset. A description of stamps or overprints where the impression has been created by the use of printer's loose type.

Typewriter Stamp. A provisional stamp produced partly or wholly on a typewriter.

Typography. Descriptive of any printing process where the design to be printed is the raised part of the plate. In typography engraving the unwanted parts of the plate area cut away, known as en épargne. Also known as letterpress or surface printing.

Ultra Violet (UV). A special light source giving off invisible radiation which activates phosphor and fluorescent substances. UV lamps are of great use to philatelists (see *Quartz lamp*).

Uncatalogued. A stamp or variety which has not been included in the major appropriate catalogue. This may be because it has not been substantiated and is possibly a forgery or reprint, or if it is a major variety because it has been discovered since the catalogue went to press.

Under Print. 1) Matter printed on the back of the stamp which may be for security, publicity or even religious purposes. 2) An all-over pattern printed on stamp paper prior to the stamp being printed either for security or decorative reasons.

Undivided Back. Descriptive of an early picture postcard when only the address was allowed to be written on the blank side. After 1897 the regulations were altered to allow this side to be used for messages as well, and a division was made so that the address space, on the right, was properly indicated (see *Divided back*).

Ungummed. A stamp without any adhesive on the back. This may be because the stamps were issued that way in the first place, or because the gum has been removed by soaking or other means at a later date (see *Unused*).

Uniform Penny Postage. The system of charging for postage introduced by Sir Rowland Hill in 1840 whereby letters were charged postage according to weight and not distance. Thus any letter falling in the first weight step could be sent anywhere within the United Kingdom for the prepayment of the one penny postage fee.

Union Jacks. A name sometimes given to the design in the upper corners of the first issues of Great Britain, the Penny Black, Red and Twopenny Blue (see *Stars*).

Unique. A term used to indicate that only one example of the stamp, tête bêche pair or other variety is known, though others are presumed to exist or have existed.

Unissued. A stamp prepared for use but never officially sold over the post office counter for any purpose.

Universal Postal Union (UPU). An organisation founded at the Berne Conference in 1874 which is responsible for the rationalisation of international arrangements between member countries including such adjustment payments as are necessary, distribution of specimen stamps to members etc.

Universal or UPU Colours. At the convention of 1898 it was agreed that members would adopt the same basic colour for stamps performing the same function and this was related to the gold standard thus:

Green: five centimes on the gold standard for first step printed papers.

Red: ten centimes on the gold standard for international postcards.

Blue: twenty-five centimes on the gold standard for single rate letters.

This system fell by the wayside as more countries left the gold standard in the 1930s and 1940s and it was finally discontinued after 1st July 1953.

Unmounted Mint (UM). A mint stamp having full gum which bears neither hinge nor hinge mark. Synonymous with "mint, never hinged", "unhinged mint".

Unofficial. A term for anything not authorised by the postal authorities. It may apply to stamps issued by private individuals or organisations (see *locals*); to overprints or underprints; to perforations or rouletting etc. Many unofficial experiments such as Henry Archer's perforation have led to official adoption at a later date.

Unpriced. A stamp listed in a catalogue but for which no price has been quoted. This usually applies to items which are rarely on the market and for which no market price is available.

Unsold. Describes an auction lot for which no bids have been received. Depending upon the auctioneer's terms and the vendor's instructions, such lots may be available for offer during the week following the sale, may be put up again in a future auction (possibly with a revised estimate) or merely withdrawn and returned to the vendor. Some auctioneers make a nominal charge on unsold lots in lieu of not receiving any commission on the sale.

Unsorted. A term indicating that the box or accumulation of stamps is as received and in effect may contain anything within the description given, nothing having been removed. It probably only truly applies to stamps coming from a prime source since once the box has changed hands two or three times, whilst still unsorted, i.e. a higgledy-piggledy mess, it may well have been picked and better items removed. Sometimes the word "unpicked" is used to indicate that this has not happened (see *Bank lot, Kiloware, Accumulation*).

Unused. Dealers' and auctioneers' term for a stamp having no cancellation upon it or gum on the back. Such stamps may have been through the post and failed to receive a cancellation, or may be mint stamps which have been cleaned up. Sometimes used for a mint stamp in poor condition or with very little gum remaining.

Collectors generally place less value on these than on either mint or used specimens and common practice on a more expensive stamp is to relate the price to the lesser of the two catalogue figures.

Used. A stamp with a cancellation confirming that it has been used for the purpose for which it was intended. If it has been used for some other authorised purpose the term will be modified to indicate this fact: for example "fiscally used" for a postage stamp used for fiscal purpose, or "postally used" for a fiscal used for postal purposes.

The term used will be further defined to describe the condition of the stamp and its cancellation or postmark. This will influence its value. Usually the following terms are used but the demarcation between each is very subjective.

Poor Used (PU): heavy cancellation, possibly with defects. Not much design visible.

Average Used (AvU): the vast majority of stamps of the issue look like this.

Good Used (GU): better than average with clear cancellation, perhaps a bit heavy, or a light cancellation a bit smudgy, covering an unimportant part of the design.

Fine Used (FU): better than good with a light clear cancellation clear of important parts of the design.

Very Fine Used (VFU): better than fine with a light clear *circular date stamp* clear of important parts of the design.

Superb Used: reserved only for the very finest copies.

Used Abroad. A stamp with postmarks or on cover used in a country other than its own, and having postal validity. Many colonies used the stamps of the mother country prior to issuing their own stamps and such usage is also "used abroad". Many collectors form *forerunner* collections of stamps used abroad in the country they collect.

Value. 1) The face value at which a stamp was sold over the post office counter. 2) The worth of a stamp in the philatelic market i.e. what a *buyer* will pay. 3) "Values" in the plural is used in descriptions, such as the number of values in a set, high values, low values etc.

Value Converted. a term used to describe Mexican stamps whose value was raised (i.e. converted) in line with the new currency by means of an overprinted symbol (see *surcharge*).

Value inserted. Stamps on which the value was inserted by hand prior to issue.

Value Tablet. On some stamps the value may be placed in a separate box or other surround and this would be known as the value tablet. Some stamps have the value tablet printed from a separate plate (the *duty plate*) and in a different colour from the rest of the stamp.

Values To. An expression used by dealers and auctioneers to indicate that the lot being described is not a complete set, but merely contains a range of values in the set up to the value quoted (see *Set to*).

Van Ackers. A popular name for the Belgium stamps whose face value was reduced by a surcharge of minus 10% in 1946, named after the country's premier of the day.

Vanguard. French security printers well known for their pioneering work with heliogravure.

Variety. Stamps having some omission from or addition to, the original design caused by an error or fault in the plate-making or printing process. Collectors differentiate between constant plate varieties which appear on the same stamp of every sheet printed from that plate; and non-constant varieties caused by the temporary introduction of some foreign body during the printing. Varieties of omission would also include missing colours, particularly where a significant part of the design such as the value or vignette was lost. 1) In modern high-speed printing methods many tiny dots and marks, very often of a constant nature, appear on stamps, though not of great significance. Such marks are known as "fly-specks" and collectors who make collections of them are knowns as "fly-speck collectors". 2) In a catalogue the term is generally used to indicate a change of colour, paper or perforation or some other significant feature. 3) In dealer's packet or auction terminology "good variety" indicates that there are many different issues or countries contained in the lot described.

Vending Machine Stamps. Stamps made up either in coils (rolls) or special booklets and which may be brought from automatic vending (coin in the slot) machines.

Views. See *Sydney Views*.

Vignette. 1) A feature or portrait in which the edges or background shades off into the paper. The technique is very often used to disguise the gaps between parts of the design printed in different colours or from two plates. 2) The central feature of a stamp design, very often a portrait. 3) The small picture on the front of an *undivided back* picture postcard which left space for a message to be written. 4) A word used to describe stamp-like labels or *etiquettes* having no face-value, particularly when seen on cover, to contrast them with the postage stamps.

"V" Mail Service. Special airmail service operating in 1942 for United States' servicemen. Similar to the *British Airgraph Service*.

Walsall Security Printers. Printers of postage stamps

particularly noted for the free-form self-adhesive and gold coin stamps of Sierra Leone and Tonga.

Wants List. A list compiled by collectors of the stamps for which they are looking and which is given to a dealer. Should the dealer come across any copies he will offer them on approval to the collector. Wants lists usually show the catalogue numbers from a recognised catalogue for the country or issue concerned.

War Stamp. A stamp produced during the wartime. It may be a propaganda stamp publicising the war effort or for fund raising; a normal stamp suitably overprinted or surcharged; or a specially printed issue, sometimes smaller in size or printed in lighter colours.

Waterlow and Sons. Famous British security printers, who have been printing stamps since 1852.

Waterlow Brothers and Layton. Printers of the first issue of the Great Britain *Seahorses*.

Watermark. A security device or design incorporated in the paper during manufacture and produced by passing the wet pulp under the *dandy roller* under pressure. The result is that the paper is slightly thinner where the watermark appears. The watermark is usually clearly visible when the paper is held up in front of the light.

Watermarks are normally upright in relation to the design of the stamp and are variously described as inverted, sideways or reversed when not in this relationship. Originally watermarks on stamp paper were produced so that one watermark design occurred centrally on each stamp, but later they occurred in a multiple all-over form so that parts of several watermarks fell on one stamp. Sometimes sheet watermarked paper in which the watermark design occurred only once in the whole sheet was used. Many countries have ceased to use watermarked paper for stamp production. Watermarks in their various designs are well illustrated in the appropriate catalogues to which the reader is referred.

Wavy Lines. A description of the pattern of lines on modern machine cancellations and generally abhorred by collectors. When they only are visible on a stamp they are the modern equivalent of a dumb cancellation since there is no means of determining where the stamp was posted.

Way Letter. A letter which was collected by the postman and delivered literally "on his way" i.e. on his round. It would not even necessarily go through the local sorting office. Such a letter was normally manually endorsed or postmarked to indicate this fact.

Weak. A term indicating that part of a stamp design, whilst not damaged, may be noticably thinner or lighter than the same part of the design on other copies of the same stamp. This usually occurs at the corners, due perhaps to uneven pressure on the transfer die or some other factor in the plate-making process.

Web. A name given to any printing process where the paper comes in continuous form from a reel and is only guillotined into sheets after the printing has taken place.

Whitebacks. A term used for specific issues of British Colonies' stamps printed on paper having a coloured surface and a white back. The paper was used to fill a gap caused by the closure of the mill supplying the original coloured papers.

Widow Weeds. A popular name for the two stamps issued in 1893 by Canada portraying Queen Victoria in her mourning clothes.

Wilding. A popular name for the first Queen Elizabeth II *definitives* of Great Britain issued in 1953. So called because the head of the queen was based on the portrait by Dorothy Wilding. During their currency they were issued with three different watermarks, experimental graphite lines, phosphor bands and different papers, and are a popular collecting group.

Wing Margin or Wing Copy. A stamp having a much wider margin on one side than the other. This happens when the *panes* of a sheet were divided by perforating down the centre of the *gutter margin* instead of down each side next to the edges of the stamp.

Withdrawn. Stamps which have been on sale at post offices may be withdrawn for a number of reasons. Sometimes, as with *commemoratives*, they were available for a limited period only, sometimes as a result of changes in postal rates a particular value is no longer required. Withdrawn commemoratives or special issues may continue to be available through the philatelic counters until stocks have been exhausted or until they are fully withdrawn, usually one year after the first date of issue. Stocks remaining when an issue is finally withdrawn should be destroyed (see *Remainders*). Withdrawn stamps may still be used for postage until they are *demonetised*.

Woodblock. A popular name or description applied to some primitives printed from wood engraved plates or *master die* (see *Xylography*). The most famous were issued in the Cape of Good Hope.

Woodstock. Reference to the "Woodstock Catalogue" which deals in great detail only with the Queen Elizabeth II stamps of Great Britain.

Worn Impression or Plate. A term used to describe a stamp having poorly printed designs due to the plate being worn from use. In any process where pressure is applied, and particularly so in printing where the plates are continually being wiped of ink etc., wear is bound to occur. The extent will depend upon the metal used for the plate. The effect on the printed design can be followed, wear usually occurring on the frame line and edges and the lighter parts first.

Wove Paper. Paper whose grain has no particular directional pattern, made by using a very fine grade wire gauze or wire mesh in the production process. Regarded as the "normal" paper for stamp production.

Wreck Cover. A cover which has been salvaged from a crashed aircraft, sunken ship etc., usually bearing evidence of the disaster. An appropriate *cachet* may have been applied giving details of the accident including date and name of the ship etc. These covers are eagerly sought after by collectors (see *Crash cover*).

Write Away. A picture postcard already having the opening words of a message printed on it.

Xylography. Printing by engraving on wood. The original engraving may be used either for direct printing or for the reproduction of impressions to make up a printing plate.

Yacht Type. A popular name for the design of stamps used in German Colonies after 1900 which features the imperial yacht *Hohenzollern*.

Year Pack. A pack issued by various countries which contain all the *commemorative* and special issues made in the country during the designated year with background information (see *Presentation pack*).

Yvert and Tellier-Champion (Y & T). the main catalogue published in France which covers French colonial stamps in detail, as well as the stamps of the rest of the world.

Zemstov Posts. Local or rural posts which operated with official approval in Russian areas not covered by the Russian Imperial Post from 1864 until the Revolution. Many issued their own stamps printed by a variety of methods, and used various cancellations in addition to pen or pencil marks.

Z Grill. The name given to one of the grills applied to stamps of USA between 1867 and 1870 as a security measure.

Zig-Zag Roulette. A type of *roulette* in which the blades are set at angles across the direction of the separation. The effect when the stamps are separated is to produce sharp pointed teeth which look fairly similar to normal perforation. Known also as serrated roulette or percé en pointes.

Zincography. A special form of relief or litho printing in which the plate is made of zinc.

Zip Code. An American term for the post code which forms part of the address to aid sorting the mail.

Zumstein (Zum). The catalogue of European stamps published by Zumstein and Cie, in Berne, Switzerland together with the specialised catalogue of Switzerland and Liechtenstein.